THE WAVES

THE WAVES

Kang Shin-jae

Translated by
TINA L. SALLEE

KEGAN PAUL INTERNATIONAL
London and New York

First published in 1989 by Kegan Paul International Limited
PO Box 256, London WC1B 3SW

Distributed by
International Thomson Publishing Services Ltd
North Way, Andover, Hants SP10 5BE
England

Routledge, Chapman and Hall Inc
29 West 35th Street
New York, NY 10001
USA

The Canterbury Press Pty Ltd
Unit 2, 71 Rushdale Street
Scoresby, Victoria 3179
Australia

Set in Times 10/12pt
by Columns of Reading
and printed in Great Britain
by T.J. Press

Korean Culture Series: edited by Chung Chong-wha
ISBN 07103 0281–9

Chapter One
SPRING

1

The wind from the sea always felt soft and sticky. For nearly
four months the ground had been frozen; now it prepared to
yield to the gentle kiss of the soft seawind that heralded the
return of the new season. Every once in a while, pale rays of
the sun timidly broke through the wind-blown grey clouds and
lit up the wintry, lead-coloured sea, turning it a glistening jade
green. Then the small, sturdy, compact houses, clustered at
the base of the hillside, took on a warm, peaceful appearance.
However, the sun's rays lingered only momentarily; soon the
sky was overcast again, spreading gloom over the whole
village.

The wind from the sea had swept away every particle of soil,
every grain of sand, from the pebble stones littering the
ground, leaving them swept clean.

Young-sil, sitting on the worn-out veranda by the wooden
floor, gazed at the rugged, uneven mountain range bordering
the town on the east. The mountain tops were covered with
tall, dark green pine trees. The mountain range extended far
beyond the shopping area, which beckoned with shimmering,
fancy lights at night, and even some miles past the quay.

Inns like miniature castles stood in a row along the
wharfside. The buildings on the street were dark and dismal,
yet seemed to be more solidly built than the inns by the quay.

1

The town, extending shapelessly in great length, eventually reached the sea, where a Japanese steamer sailed to and from Shinho, and countless small steamboats plied the waters in a leisurely way as far as the horizon. If you crossed the main road where the brothels – deserted during the day – nestled at the foot of the mountain, you would clearly hear the ship's piercing whistle right behind you, its enormous vibration jarring your ears.

Opposite the busy waterfront stretched a panorama of white sandy beaches. The west side of town was completely closed-in by a bare and rocky mountain, devoid of trees, ugly and even threatening. Its name was Chunma which means 'heavenly horse'. Intimidated by its sinister appearance, children were afraid to climb it.

Gazing at the mountain, Young-sil was lost in thought. 'I believe the leper still lives in that mountain. The one who kidnapped the police detective-in-chief's child last spring and took out his liver and ate it raw.' Instinctively, Young-sil rearranged her posture, bringing her swaying legs together and sat tightly. 'I heard rumours that the leper ate the child's liver and left the child leaning against a tree. People can still hear it crying for its mother from the mountain. "I want my mummy. Mummy, mummy!"'

This terrifying thought made her tiny body tremble violently. The whole episode of the crime of the leper and the tragedy of the child was too horrible for her to accept. Yet, in spite of her fears Young-sil was possessed with an unshakeable desire to go to the mountain again when the azaleas were in full bloom. She could not forget the thrilling feeling of picking armfuls of pink azaleas in the heart of the deep mountain, gathering more and more flowers until her hands were completely buried under the blossoms.

The bluebell season had the same effect on her. These too gave her a restless yearning to pick them. Sometimes drifts of bluebells would cover the entire slope, their tiny petals like precious pearls and their rich, penetrating fragrance delighting her senses.

'Let's go home,' her friend would urge rather nervously. 'I think we have enough flowers now.' She was ready to leave, but Young-sil was still not satisfied. She kept walking further up the mountain, ignoring her friend's suggestion. Young-sil loved to feel the mysterious stillness of the mountain; its daytime quiet fascinated her. Only the occasional calls of courting birds penetrated its stillness and the wholesome mountain air filled her senses with its sweetness and freshness.

'Look!' someone cried. 'I can see the leper over there!' There was always someone frivolous among the group of girls who came to pick flowers with her.

'Where?' Young-sil asked in alarm.

'I saw something white pass by quickly right behind the tree,' her friend replied, gasping with fright. 'Can't you hear someone crying?'

'No,' Young-sil shook her head. 'Where is the crying coming from?'

'Over there! Can't you hear it?'

'It's only a cuckoo,' Young-sil insisted.

Although Young-sil managed to convince her friend she was mistaken, she herself was seized by fear of the leper. When she tried to take a step to leave the place right away, she found it difficult to walk with her arms full of flowers. Reluctantly, in order to walk freely, she had to give up most of the beautiful flowers she had picked so eagerly.

Young-sil narrowed her eyes as she remembered. 'The sticky wind from the sea may be too harsh yet to breathe,' she thought, 'but it surely heralds the approach of spring. Soon I'll be able to go to the mountain again.'

Slightly cramped from crouching on the hard surface of the veranda, Young-sil slowly stepped down onto the courtyard and stretched herself fully. She looked nervously around in all directions. Her eyes rested on the narrow road leading directly from her house to the hilltop. The road stretched out in front of the main gate, in the shape of a letter T. Compared with its length, the road was conspicuously elevated and consequently, had the appearance of an elevated bridge. Its surface had been worn away over the years by the harsh, cruel weather, smoothed by countless steps; however, its smoothness was interrupted by large, round stones held firmly in place in the road bed. At both edges of the road were round holes where children loved to play, lowering their bodies into the holes and climbing in and out.

Young-sil could clearly see the small precipice over her low front gate. A small woman, dressed in cream and carrying water buckets strapped to her back, was cautiously climbing the slope. The woman was Young-sil's mother. Because she believed the water from all the wells in the neighbourhood too salty to drink, she used to go all the way to the opposite hill to fetch water for her family.

With each strong gust of the wind, the rectangular water buckets, dangling from each end of the long stick supported on her shoulder, leaned to one side, swaying at will. Although Young-sil's mother tried hard to balance herself by pushing her head and chest forward with all her might, the powerful breath of the north wind frustrated her efforts. She was repeatedly forced to stand still for a moment, and sometimes the wind forced her to step back against her will.

Young-sil smiled as she watched her mother's struggle. Now she was drawing nearer to the house. Her mother looked much younger than her age, even though a few wrinkles were discernible here and there on her face. Perhaps the secret of her youthful looks was her tranquil nature. She always seemed to be cheerful and carefree.

A sudden, strong gust of wind caused an uncontrollable commotion to the water buckets. Young-sil's mother's hair blew about aimlessly and her long skirt, which was securely held round her waist by a belt, fluttered freely. Without any warning Young-sil's mother was mercilessly thrown to the foot of the slope. Her tiny body was blown away together with the water buckets dangling from her shoulders. In haste, Young-sil dashed to the rescue. The buckets were making a clamorous sound as they were hurled along and water from the buckets began to flow along the road. Her mother landed like a crumpled doll at the foot of the precipice, still supporting the long stick on her shoulders. She scrambled to her feet and blinked her eyes in a dazed fashion as if she were dizzy. Young-sil could not help bursting out laughing, showing her well-set, white teeth, at her mother's confused look.

'Mother, you look just like a cat,' she giggled. 'Just like a frightened cat!' Her laughing face, flushed with youthful vitality, was startlingly attractive. Her features – dark skin, large eyes, small nose and close-lipped, firm mouth – did not immediately impress others as pretty, and in fact, Young-sil regarded herself as plain and unattractive. However, her face radiated the freshness of youth, and she had the look of a dauntless boy full of vitality, spirit and gallantry.

Young-sil's mother lifted her head swiftly and turned to see what had happened to her water pails. As soon as she spotted them, she scurried over to pick them up, skilfully rehanging them on each ring of the water carrier.

Young-sil's sister, Sinn-sil, walked briskly into the courtyard through the back door, and asked in a low voice, 'What has happened to Mother, Young-sil?' Slight creases between her eyebrows suggested some kind of hidden anxiety as if she were worried about something. Unlike her younger sister, Sinn-sil was a striking beauty. Her loveliness and womanly charm were greatly admired by everyone around her. In the light-coloured blouses she loved to wear, Sinn-sil was truly as lovely as a full-blossomed peony in springtime. Her fair complexion, double eyelids, and rosy cheeks made her very desirable. She gave the impression of being gentle, amiable, docile and modest. Her loosely braided long hair was worn slightly covering the ears to signify that she was a virgin.

Not long ago, however, a vicious rumour began to follow her like a dark shadow, staining her reputation as a virtuous girl. According to gossip, Sinn-sil had been seen walking with a man near the foot of Chunma Mountain, or been caught in a rendezvous with a certain man behind the supplementary school building. At first people did not hesitate to join in the gossip, criticizing her alleged indecent behaviour, but as time passed they accepted that the rumours were groundless and that Sinn-sil was an innocent victim of slander spread out of malice. Instead of cold stares and whispered accusations, people now expressed their sympathy for Sinn-sil.

In fact judging from her character and life style, no one could believe that Sinn-sil could be so dissipated as the foolish rumour said. Most people knew her as someone morally irreproachable and physically rather fragile. Her voice was quiet and gentle and her gaze was modest; she seemed always to be lowering her eyes.

Young-sil pointed to their mother. 'She fell from the cliff, you see. Miraculously she is unhurt without a scratch – she landed on her feet, just like a cat!' Young-sil giggled again, shaking her long, bushy hair. Slowly Sinn-sil turned to look at her mother, who was standing off-balance, fingering a ring of the water carrier on her shoulders. Even though she had no idea what had happened to her mother, Sinn-sil felt it was no concern of hers. She had her own concerns. She asked no further questions but lowered her eyes and turned away. By this time her mother had started to follow the path leading back to the hilly road.

'My dear sister, don't you think Mother's face looks like a cat's?' Young-sil persisted, still laughing softly with good humour. 'Especially when she is crouching on the ground, she looks altogether just like a cat!' Sinn-sil made no reply. She walked towards the veranda by the main wooden floor. She had left her embroidery frame behind the shoe chest that was made from a wooden apple box. Now she intended to take it away to her room, which faced the backyard of the house.

'I wonder how on earth Mother managed to escape without injury when she fell from the cliff?' Young-sil abruptly stopped her silly giggling, and fell silent. Her father's dark figure appeared through the door behind the veranda. Her father's eyes, expressive of unspoken melancholy, gave people the feeling he was a man of few words. His brooding personality made people feel uncomfortable, even awestruck.

Young-sil's father, Mann-kap Shin, was even more taciturn than his wife who was very quiet by nature. Unlike her mother, however, her father gave the impression of barely restrained violence bottled up inside him, as though he would explode at the slightest touch. Young-sil was afraid of her father. She often felt terrified by him. He was a big man – husky, robust in build, and strong as a rock. It was several years now since his unexpected retirement from his lifelong vocation as a fisherman. Since then he had been jobless, always staying inside the house. No one knew what he was thinking about all the time behind his brooding eyes. No one seemed able to fathom his secretive mind. Very few people came to see him and he never engaged in a long, serious conversation with others. Nevertheless Mr Shin knew all the rumours about his elder daughter. In fact, he had reliable, accurate information about her.

He looked at his daughters out of the corner of his eyes. Even though his eyes cast daggers at her sister, Young-sil was intimidated by his glare. It made her shrink in fear. At her father's penetrating stare, Sinn-sil's head drooped listlessly. She hesitated momentarily, and then reached behind the shoe chest to get her embroidery frame. Her father's eyes flashed flame and his rage erupted. Young-sil screamed out in alarm, 'Oh, Dad, she has only been to Soon-ock's house to learn embroidery. I swear she didn't go anywhere else – she came straight home!'

Sinn-sil, turning pale, withdrew her hand from behind the shoe chest. The embroidery frame was not there.

Suddenly, her father lowered one shoulder. Before Sinn-sil could recover from her surprise, she had the further shock of seeing her beloved embroidery frame being flung out of the room onto the courtyard and smashed before her eyes.

'You'd better come with me. Get into that room this instant, girl,' her father thundered, his voice resounding like an echo in the mountains. His voice was full of fury and misery that sprang up from the depths of his soul. As if she were a piece of metal attracted by a giant magnet, Sinn-sil approached her father without resistance. When she reached the veranda, her father grabbed a handful of her hair and threw her down in a rage. He dragged her along, still holding her by the hair. As she crossed the threshold her blouse was torn apart, exposing part of her bare shoulder. As if he were inflamed by the sight of her exposed shoulder, Mr Shin became even angrier. Breathing harshly, he violently pulled her hair. The reed mat on the floor crunched under his weight as he dragged his daughter inside, into the long, narrow innermost room. Sinn-sil's tightly held hair was finally freed. Her father stepped down onto the courtyard and strode toward the twig fence in order to pick a bundle of narrow sticks. He arranged them layer by layer and then tied the bundle with a string lying nearby on the ground. Understanding her father's intention Young-sil darted like an arrow out of the door. Without pausing for breath, she raced along the road towards her mother who with stooped back was approaching, the water carrier creaking as she walked.

Young-sil screamed hysterically at her mother to come at once. She pulled the water carrier from her mother's shoulders. Her mother's brown eyes, which cast a green light up close, were fixed on her excited daughter in alarm. She started to run towards the house, leaving the water carrier.

Young-sil attempted to carry the water by herself but she was not strong enough. Its heavy weight pulled painfully at her shoulders. After taking a few, difficult steps, she gave up trying to carry the water buckets home. Without a second thought she put them down and emptied the water at the side of the road. The she hurried home, panting and puffing with the two empty pails that had been nearly blown away by the raging wind.

'Aren't you going to speak at all?' Her father's angry voice came from the innermost room, accompanying the sharp sound of a blow. 'Aren't you going to confess, girl? Where have you been? Where have you been wandering all day, hmm?'

Ignoring her father's savage attack, Sinn-sil leaned sideways, supporting herself with her hands placed firmly on the floor. Her soft, silent gaze was fixed on somewhere totally different and distant. Her large, round eyes were aloof and faraway as if she were in a dream. As if her father's outrageous shouting and screaming had nothing to do with her, as if this behaviour affected her not at all, Sinn-sil remained still and calm. However, as her thin arms were mercilessly beaten, her head suddenly drooped heavily.

Her mother, who was trembling with fright at the door, rushed to her husband, grabbed his arm and clung to it with all her might.

He stood up straight, stretching his back, and lifted his small wife and threw her out bodily onto the courtyard. As if nothing had happened, he picked up the switch again and began once more to whip his daughter. At every stroke of the whip, Young-sil trembled in fear and sympathy. At last she could endure his brutality no longer, and like a soul in torment burst into a howl of protest at her father's unjust punishment of her innocent sister.

'Oh, Father, please! She has only been to her friend's house to learn more about embroidery! What's wrong with that, Father? Is learning embroidery a crime, a sin?' Young-sil frantically defended her sister.

'Oh, my husband, please listen to me. She has been to Mr Chae's house. You know the Mr Chae the school teacher? Well, he asked Sinn-sil to come over. He said he had something urgent to tell her – something about his getting a divorce from his wife. Please believe me,' his wife cried.

'You have known all along where Sinn-sil was, Father. Why

do you keep asking her the same question when you already
know the answer yourself? Why do you keep hurting my
sister? Why, Father?' At last, Young-sil, in anger and despair,
sank her healthy, strong white teeth into her father's arm.
Sinn-sil, her eyes tightly closed, had collapsed like a dead body
on the floor that had not yet been papered.

2

'Is it true that your sister's head is completely shaved?' Soon-
hee, Young-sil's good friend asked in a grown-up manner.
Young-sil was speechless. Then, after a long pause, she shook
her head.

'No, it isn't true. It simply isn't so.' This weak denial did not
seem to convince her friend. Soon-hee shook her head gently
as if she were sorry she asked.

'Everyone in the village talks about your sister and your
father, you know,' Soon-hee said softly. 'I wonder what makes
your father so mean and cruel towards his own daughter?'

Young-sil ignored this remark and retied the cloth wrapper
that held her school books. As she rearranged the plum-
coloured cloth around her waist, the clanking of her empty
lunch box, which was also wrapped in the cloth, sounded
louder than ever.

'Do you know what I heard? Mrs Chae beat her husband
with a poker!' Soon-hee giggled. 'Mr Chae's face was all
swollen and battered this morning.'

Dark, bluish water was flowing sleekly over the rocks at the
foot of Chunma Mountain. The two girls quickened their pace
as the chirping of a mysterious bird on the mountainside
penetrated the thin air. The elementary school was quite a
distance from the village and the village children had to walk
past many unpleasant, even terrifying, places in order to get to
school. The road that led to school at the base of Chunma
Mountain was isolated and lonely. The schoolchildren had to
pass through an open field where they knew a witch lived in a
hut. They also had to face a weeping willow tree where a
certain woman hanged herself not long ago. People belived
that restless ghosts haunted this area on evenings when the
rain was falling gently. Pieces of brightly coloured cloth – red,

blue, and yellow – always tied tightly around the long, barbed wire fence behind the military police post, indicated the presence of ghosts. Scattered lumps of congealed rice and heads of dried fish in front of the huge rocks along the road also confirmed the superstition.

Every day it was getting warmer. The warm spring wind tickled the girls' cheeks pleasantly. Twilight, casting long shadows, was gradually blocked by Chunma Mountain. After sunset the road was transformed into something pale and colourless. Everything became grey and gloomy as the sun retired for the day.

'My sister is getting married to a rich man in Seoul!' abruptly Young-sil informed her friend Soon-hee.

'Marrying a rich man?' marvelled Soon-hee, blinking her eyes curiously. 'You mean someone rich like Mr Daal-soo Chang in our village?'

Soon-hee added in an insinuating whisper, 'I understand Mr Chang's oldest son is back home from Japan. He goes to college somewhere in Japan and comes home at vacation time.' Suddenly, Soon-hee stopped talking as if she had just remembered something important and gave Young-sil a side-long glance. 'I saw your sister with Mr Chang's oldest son last spring,' she exclaimed excitedly. 'I think I saw them behind the building at "Keeyomee" hot spring. You know the place – it's on the other side of the mountain.'

Young-sil sighed deeply, recalling her sister's restless wanderings last spring. 'I'm worried about my sister,' she confessed. 'She seems to have no intention of getting married and settling down. She goes to indecent places . . . I wish she wouldn't.'

'Do you wish your sister would marry Mr Chang's son, then?' Soon-hee asked with a giggle.

Mr Daal-soo Chang was a local hero. He had become a millionaire overnight with his successful fishery, and was respected and admired by all the villagers, although he probably did not know how to read or even write his own name. In spite of his illiteracy, he had a private secretary, a Japanese girl, and his office was in the Japanese merchants' section of town. Mr Chang always wore fine clothes, even a luxurious fur coat during the winter, to show how rich and important he was. Whenever he wanted to go to town, Mr

Chang would call the First Taxi Service Company and a black taxi would come rambling along to fetch him. Mr Chang was also known as a big spender – the only wealthy man in Wonjin with that reputation.

Surrounding Mr Chang's house was a long, high brick wall to protect it from burglars. His watch dog was as famous as his master. No one seemed to know what kind of breed he was. He had been bought from a Russian some time ago and resembled a lanky deer. He had no tail, which made him look rather peculiar. Every once in a while, Mr Chang's dog managed to slip out of the house and run swiftly through the streets. Whenever the dog escaped, Mr Chang's servant would risk his life chasing him through the streets until he managed to bring the dog back. Mr Chang's servant was arrogant and haughty, behaving as if he thought himself better than anybody else, and consequently much disliked by the villagers.

The name Daal-soo Chang was a symbol of wealth and power; his son was regarded and treated like a crown prince by the village girls.

'When do you think your sister will go to Seoul, Young-sil?' Soon-hee asked in a sceptical tone. Young-sil pretended to ignore her friend's question at first, finally replying curtly, 'I have no idea, to tell you the truth.' Young-sil was regretting her boast and resolved not to engage in idle talk again.

A local bus stopped at the entrance of the marketplace and two or three middle school girls in navy blue school uniforms got off. Since there was no middle school in Wonjin, girls and boys commuted every day to the neighbouring city by bus.

Upon seeing the schoolgirls, Soon-hee announced that when she went to the middle school next year, the first thing she would buy was a pair of leather shoes. Although Soon-hee had lost her mother when she was little, her father, the fire station chief, had devoted his life to her. He was determined to do his best to give his only daughter a good education, and so Soon-hee took it for granted that she would go to middle school next year. Some people liked to murmur that the big fire at the sardine cannery two years ago had sent Mr Choi out of his senses.

Young-sil knew there was no hope for her of going to middle school; in fact, she had given up all hope of being able to continue her education. Yet she was still interested in discussing with her friend the new experiences and the exciting prospect of going to middle school. In this mood, Young-sil and Soon-hee continued to chatter, feeling more at ease now.

A certain boy was approaching and from their glimpse of him, Young-sil and Soon-hee noticed that he was remarkably handsome, though apparently sad and dejected. Young-sil and Soon-hee fell silent.

Children born and brought up in small seaside towns have a tendency to mature earlier than others. It is common for girls to reach puberty as early as ten or eleven. They start to flirt with the boys, deliberately resorting to various strategies to attract their attention. They giggle and gossip about falling in love and frequently speculate about who is fancying whom.

This handsome melancholy looking boy, however, had never been a subject for gossip. In fact, he appeared to be indifferent and aloof to the other students. He never joined in their games, roamed the streets at night or chased girls into dark alleys for kicks. Village people were both irritated and anxious whenever they saw Kyung-sik Yoon on the street. He would walk straight past people, who felt sorry for his mother, keeping his chin up high and apparently unaffected by what people said or thought about him.

When Kyung-sik had passed the girls, Soon-hee was eager to resume their conversation, but Young-sil was sullen and quiet. Somehow she no longer felt like talking with her friend. She felt weary and dispirited without knowing why. With this sudden change of mood, Young-sil parted from her friend at the fire station in front of the marketplace. Soon-hee and her father lived in a small room adjoining his office at the fire station.

After leaving Soon-hee, Young-sil went home. She went to the kitchen and began to eat a bowl of cooked millet, sitting on the veranda by the fireplace. The water in the large iron pot at one end of the fireplace was not yet boiling and her mother was building up the fire.

'Young-sil, dear, why don't you try some stewed crayfish?' her mother suggested kindly, but Young-sil had little appetite.

Her sister, Sinn-sil was lying listlessly in the inner room. Sinn-sil's head had been closely shaved by her father, and Young-sil felt sorry for her, yet she was reluctant to involve herself in her sister's problems. Since the day he had shaved his daughter's head, Mr Shin had kept to himself in the back room by the side veranda.

Young-sil pushed aside the cereal bowl and went outside. She walked down the slope of the hill in the gathering dusk. At the foot of the hill, an old man lived with his son and daughter-in-law in their cottage. Every morning and evening the old man never failed to come out into the road and curse them, lifting his arms high to heaven. 'You ungrateful brats,' he would shout in disgust, 'your necks deserve to be wrung, you worthless scum! Don't you realize how many hardships your mother and I went through to raise you to become a decent human being, but now look at yourself! You are good-for-nothing.'

No one bothered to listen or respond to his grievance.

'Am I not right? Can you blame me for grumbling? My wife had a terrible time giving birth to you. We did our best to bring you up, we endured more than our share of hardship . . .' The complaints continued increasingly. The old man's grey hair accentuated his old age and feebleness; his topknot tied with remnants of loose hair was no bigger than a thumb of a child. His torn sleeve flapped wildly as he gestured with his arms.

Carrying a large wooden tray on her head his poor but dutiful daughter-in-law went silently into the house. She scooped out a handful of millet from the tray and cooked it for her father-in-law, her husband and herself. Now the son came out of the shabby hut and called his father.

'Come, Father, it's time for supper now. Please come in.' As soon as the old man heard his son's voice, he abruptly ceased his railing and slowly followed him inside.

Although every morning and evening the old man made the same scene, most of the day he usually sat on the threshold gazing at the street, chewing dried sandfish roe which his good daughter-in-law gave him. As Young-sil passed by, the old man turned his head slightly as if he were glad to see her again. Usually Young-sil didn't mind talking to the lonely old man, who would sometimes delight her with an unexpected response. However, today she did not feel like speaking to him, and passed by, ignoring him completely.

Without knowing why, Young-sil was distracted and confused, unable to control her extraordinary feelings. At first she

13

blamed her sister for her state of mind; then she felt that perhaps the schoolboy, Kyung-sik Yoon, whom she had passed on the way home from school, was even more to blame for her nervous and uneasy mood. Always, whenever she was troubled or disturbed, there was one particular place which would calm her down. Young-sil took the wider path at the fork of the rough road leading in different directions from the post office on the main street. There were some houses, a general store, and a dispensary of Chinese medicine along the road. At the top of the hill lived her friend Sung-aah. Her house was painted jade green. It was called the 'Seoul Clinic'. Over the entrance the small triangular roof looked elegant, and the crisp, white curtains, hung at each window, increased Young-sil's admiration for the entire house. Even the principal at school was not privileged enough to have curtains in his office. The church had large, dark, drab pieces of cloth as curtains, but they were shabby, shapeless and torn here and there. The ugly black curtains were used as a stage curtain for plays during the winter months.

Sung-aah's father, Dr Baek, was renowned throughout the town for his fine surgical skills. Once he had successfully operated on a child with a ruptured intestine. Another time Dr Baek saved a country woman who had been almost beaten to death by her daughter-in-law's brother. The woman had been so harsh and cruel to her daughter-in-law that she had driven her to commit suicide. In grief and furious revenge the brother of the young woman attacked the mother-in-law with a hoe in a dark room until, according to rumour, her face was so swollen that no trace of her nose, eyes or mouth could be seen.

Sung-aah's mother talked pleasantly and aimably, using only the dialect of Seoul. Her hair was always neatly rolled up and she wore a fine hair net. The living room area was always bright and tidy. The floor of each room was covered with laminated paper. What impressed Young-sil most in her friend's house was that in every room were always plenty of fresh fruit and biscuits. In well-to-do Japanese homes, Young-sil supposed, such extravagance might be quite normal, but in a Korean home it was extraordinary. Secretly Young-sil envied her friend's life style. Indeed, Sung-aah was quite different from any of her other friends, and very special in Young-sil's eyes.

14

Sung-aah had been transferred to Young-sil's school from another city the previous autumn. Unlike most new pupils, Sung-aah was not nervous or shy. Indeed, she seemed relaxed and poised in her new environment, at peace with herself. She was neither impudent nor conceited but behaved naturally to everyone. In addition to her charming personality, Sung-aah was much admired as an outstanding student. She was keenly perceptive and blessed with an amazing good memory. In Young-sil's eyes, Sung-aah was an exceptionally gifted person.

Not long after Sung-aah joined Young-sil's class, the annual Japanese festival day approached. It fell on a Sunday that year.

'Children, tomorrow each of you should visit the shrine to pay your respects. Do you understand?' the home-room teacher announced. Although all the children nodded their heads emphatically none of them intended to visit the sacred shrine as instructed.

The shrine was located in a secluded spot, quite a distance away from the waterfront. It always appeared dark and gloomy; consequently, it was not a place any child wanted to visit alone. Because of its isolated and dreary atmosphere, even the teachers who had dutifully encouraged them to visit the shrine did not expect any of the children actually to go there.

The festival day turned out cold and dreary. The wind howled and brought a sudden chill, and the sea in the distance turned grey and nasty, breaking savagely. The restless waves were driven by the raging storm. Such weather was intimidating and vicious enough to discourage any kind of outing.

Early that morning, Young-sil had discovered that Sung-aah had actually gone to the shrine. She was the only one foolish enough to follow the teacher's futile instructions. Young-sil found her new friend's innocence rather amusing and decided to return that evening to tease her about her well-meant visit to the shrine.

'You know, you didn't really have to go,' Young-sil laughed at her friend. 'Nobody expects anyone to go, you silly.'

'Perhaps you're right, Young-sil,' Sung-aah said in a matter-of-fact tone. 'No one showed up but me.'

'Whatever made you go to the shrine in this cold, windy weather? It's such a long way away.' Young-sil scolded her over and over again, quivering her nostrils. She was enjoying teasing her friend.

'I'm glad I went,' declared Sung-aah softly, smiling. 'I felt very good there. Even the sound of the wind and waves were different – mysterious, even. I would love to go there again.' Sung-aah sounded as if she meant what she had said. Young-sil didn't think Sung-aah was trying to mislead her.

'Tomorrow, if our teacher doesn't ask who has been to the shrine, will you be disappointed, Sung-aah?'

'What do you mean by "disappointed"?' Sung-aah asked, opening her eyes wider as if she didn't get the hidden meaning of her friend's remark. 'Perhaps I may be a little disappointed; but let me tell you something. I'm really glad I went to the shrine. It gave me a sense of discovery, of finding something new inside me. Can you understand what I mean?'

Young-sil found herself at a loss. Sung-aah's statement surprised her. She could not fully comprehend Sung-aah's profound feelings. She could understand to some extent, yet she was confused. In this frame of mind, Young-sil made up her mind to take Sung-aah to the mountain when spring came with its fanciful array of pink azaleas along the mountain ridges.

Sung-aah was always reserved. Because of her personality, she sometimes gave the impression of being cold and aloof. However, she had always been kind and pleasant with Young-sil, who was very outgoing and talkative. Sung-aah rarely revealed her inner feelings, while Young-sil loved to talk about herself. Sung-aah waited for others to make the first move; not out of pride or conceit, but because of her introverted nature.

Thinking about Sung-aah and their friendship, Young-sil paused in front of her house, then entered by a small gate at the entrance. She walked around the house inside the outer wall and entered the front courtyard where Sung-aah's mother greeted her.

'Come on in, Young-sil, dear. Sung-aah is in the room just across the hall.'

Young-sil was flattered to be greeted so warmly by Sung-aah's mother, for Korean villagers rarely speak to children. They seem to ignore their existence except when they scold them for misbehaviour or tell them to do something.

16

Consequently, children do not greet, or expect to be greeted by, their elders. They do not even say 'How do you do?' when they happen to meet an adult. Whenever a child visits his friend, he goes inside quietly and if his friend is not at home, he goes out as quickly as he came in, without bothering to ask questions.

Sung-aah's home was different. Young-sil was made to feel at home whenever she visited her friend.

As soon as she heard where Sung-aah was, Young-sil went into her room and found her reading a children's book. Young-sil was very impressed with the book which delighted her with its colourful illustrations.

'May I read with you?' Young-sil asked.

'Of course, you may. Here's a book for you,' Sung-aah extended her invitation immediately. As Young-sil sat close by her friend, she could smell an unpleasant odour coming from her body. In embarrassment and sudden shame, she stretched her skirt down to her feet. While they were deeply absorbed in the books, a maid came into the room with lots of biscuits on a tray. Sung-aah grinned when she saw the biscuits.

'What's so funny?' Young-sil wanted to know.

'It's these,' Sung-aah pointed to the biscuits. 'Whenever we have these Japanese biscuits, the old man, whom we call Koobae's grandfather, comes without fail. Isn't that funny? You wait and see, then you'll find out what I mean.'

Although Young-sil had no idea what her friend was talking about, she burst out laughing too.

'I wonder why he likes this kind so much. And how does he know when you have his favourite biscuits when he's not even in the room?'

'Maybe he has a keen sense of smell. But I know one thing for sure, he'll soon be here.'

While they were chattering and giggling, they heard a dry cough in the next room.

'That's him all right,' Sung-aah exclaimed excitedly, and she and Young-sil burst into uncontrollable laughter.

'What's going on in here, girls?' asked Sung-aah's mother, who had entered the room to put something away in a wooden cabinet that was inlaid with mother-of-pearl. When she saw the dish of Japanese biscuits, Sung-aah's mother began to laugh too.

Whenever the old man, Koo-bae's grandfather, was eating his favourite Japanese biscuits, Young-sil's face turned crimson as she tried to stifle her laugher. He was pockmarked and so old that his lower chin was bent inward like a spoon for scooping rice. The shiny, deep-tanned skin, which covered his large joints, showed good health and vitality for his age. His eyes sparkled, indicating his mental alertness.

According to rumour, he had never fished for his living, but spent most of his younger days travelling on the high sea. He used to take anything available – fishing boats, small steamships, or large freighters – to go in search of his fortune in strange and distant places. He had endured many hardships and calamities during his wanderings, and in spite of his constant seeking, he never found what he was looking for. As a last resort he came to this strange harbour city in the north, far away from his hometown in Pyung-ahn Province, and decided to settle down. Now he lived with his poor diligent son and his family on the top of the mountain.

'Please tell us a story, sir,' Sung-aah begged. He was a good storyteller, with many fascinating tales to tell about his extraordinary experiences in different places. Consequently, his tales transcended all others in appeal.

'Story? What kind of story are you talking about, girl?' He pretended not to understand, a frequent ploy of his.

'Oh, you know, one of your fascinating stories! Please tell us one,' Sung-aah pleaded, pushing the biscuit dish in front of him. The dish of Japanese biscuits was nearly consumed by the time he consented to comply with her friendly request.

Young-sil took full advantage of this rare opportunity to observe the old man closely, never having seen him so close before.

'Any of your stories will do,' Sung-aah's grandmother encouraged him, smiling. 'Just tell us one of your adventures, please!' Sung-aah's grandmother had an oval-shaped face which lit up with warmth and geniality. Her head was always covered with a silk scarf. Since breaking her left arm when she fell on the ice on the way to church one wintry night she kept it supported with her right hand all the time. The wide gold ring on her left index finger received her constant attention as if it were her most precious treasure.

She had spent most of her life in Seoul and Pyungyang; consequently, it had been hard for her to adjust to life in this strange fishing village. She found this northern port very difficult to live in – with its fierce wind all year round, rough, harsh village people and the dreary, cold weather even in springtime, she felt no special affection or attachment to this alien environment.

Since she had nothing in common with her neighbours, Sung-aah's grandmother was often lonely and for this reason she was glad to have the old man, Koo-bae's grandfather, for company. They both came from the same province, which made her feel at home with him. She looked forward to his occasional visits and enjoyed talking with him.

'Story? What kind of story would you like to hear today?' he asked, patting his thighs gently and tilting his torso sideways.

'Please tell us the story of how you managed to pull out your tooth,' pleaded Sung-aah, determined to have him tell Young-sil a story that she herself found very funny and comical.

'Oh, yes, I'll tell you that one again.' The old man grinned as if he were well-pleased with all the attention he was receiving.

'One day I had a terrible toothache,' the old man began his story. 'The pain was so severe that I decided to extract it right away. So I shook it hard and tried to pull it out, but it wouldn't come out as I had hoped, even though it was loose.' The old man leant over to one side. Whenever he tilted the upper part of his body like this, a delightful mood spread throughout the room making everyone full of joyful anticipation.

'The tooth was driving me crazy; so at last I tied a length of strong thread around it and tied the other end to my big toe. Then, I sat down, trying to pull it out,' the old man explained with gestures to suit his words.

'My effort was in vain. The stubborn tooth still wouldn't come out, you see.' He picked up his favourite biscuit as if he needed to supplement his energy. With a rapid movement of his sunken chin, shaped like a soup ladle, he greedily consumed the whole biscuit. Young-sil and her friend watched fascinated.

'So I had to try another method,' he continued. 'This time I tied a piece of string tightly to the head of a hammer. Then I looked around for something I could nail with that hammer. Guess what I found? A shelf! Its support was dangling, ready to drop, you see. It was the perfect place to use the hammer; so I hammered with all my strength. I repaired the shelf's support all right!'

'What happened to your tooth?' Young-sil asked excitedly. 'Did it come out?'

'Yes, it certainly did.'

'Did you bleed much?'

'Yes, I did.'

'What happened to the shelf?'

'It was fixed nicely.'

'You mean you used your hammer only once to fix that support?'

'I used it several times, my girl,' the old man replied, satisfied. 'The tooth was dangling at the end of the string.'

Sung-aah merely smiled as the old man finished his story but her grandmother, rubbing her weak left arm, frowned disapprovingly as if she were disgusted by his tale.

'Why don't you tell us about the night you spent at the empty house?' Sung-aah asked eagerly. Without a second thought, flattered to be asked again, the old man launched into a second story enthusiastically.

'It was drizzling that evening,' he began. 'Not many people lived in Wonjin at that time. You could easily count the houses throughout the entire area. Anyway, this place used to be a mountain trail. Nobody lived there then, so on any snowy day the hungry wolves would come down to the trail.

'The sea looked wild and frightening when I saw it from the top of the hill. I cursed myself for ending up in a place like this – isolated and unfriendly. There was not a single boat available for me to take, and my travel funds were all gone. I was at the end of the line. I couldn't stay or leave this godforsaken place.

'In desperation, I decided to look for work, any kind of work, on the waterfront next morning. So I tried to find a place to spend the night, but I couldn't find any. In despair, I found myself walking towards the pub which was in the centre of the village then, you see.

'Please forgive me, ma'am, for mentioning it, but back then, I was too weak to resist the temptation of strong drink.'

20

Sung-aah's grandmother, a devout, pious Christian, nodded her head graciously as if she had compassion for this sinful creature, as if she had forgiven his iniquities.

'I asked the landlady for something to eat in exchange for my jacket,' the old man went on. 'She gave me a bowl of hot beef soup with rice. They called her Bukchung Auntie. She may not have been a Christian, but she was a good woman. She refused my offer to pay for my food with my jacket. What do you think of that?'

Young-sil moved closer to the old man. She was enthralled. The woman, 'Bukchung Auntie', was still managing a small bar somewhere in town. Her son was a notorious juvenile delinquent.

'Bukchung Auntie' always wore a sordid, greasy old apron round her waist. She yelled all day long at her son, who was not at all like her. People wondered how in the world she, who was big and heavy, came to have such a flawlessly handsome boy whose long, thick eyelashes accentuated his clean appearance. Some whispered that he was not her son at all but had been born to a barmaid who used to work for 'Bukchung Auntie'. However, he had been brought up as her own son. Now he squandered her money and skipped his classes as frequently as he could. In spite of all his weakness and shortcomings, 'Bukchung Auntie' treated him as if he were of noble birth.

'What happened after you finished your soup?'

'Oh, yes! Upon finishing my tasty soup,' the old man went on eagerly, 'I asked Bukchung Auntie where I could spend the night.'

'My dear man, you had such nerve,' Sung-aah's grandmother declared admiringly as if she were impressed. 'You must have been quite brave; otherwise, you couldn't have come to a place like this all alone. You see I came here with my son and his family and live very comfortably. But I still haven't managed to get accustomed to this town yet.'

'She couldn't find a proper place for me,' the old man continued. 'So she suggested I should go to the church and see if they could help. Seeing that I was at a loss, a guy next to me got up clumsily and announced he would be happy to show me where I could sleep that night. He was so drunk that he could hardly open his eyes, and he kept losing his balance.'

21

Suddenly the old man turned his head, looking closely at Young-sil and Sung-aah. At this unexpected attention to them, the girls moved closer to him.

'Bukchung Auntie tried to persuade me not to go out with the drunkard, but I went with him into the drizzling night and followed him for some time until I was led to a hill. After we climbed the hill in pitch darkness, he asked me whether I could see the huge house on the hilltop. I nodded. The house was all by itself, and the drunkard told me it was haunted. He explained that the house was built on a gravesite, and that's why it was haunted. Many people had tried to live in that haunted house, but no one had succeeded, he said. He told me that I could easily catch the ghost, that I looked strong enough to knock down any kind of ghost. And then he turned and started to climb back down to the main road.'

'Have you ever seen that man again?' Sung-aah asked anxiously.

'No, my dear girl, I've never seen him since. He gave me the impression he was a sailor. Anyway, if I see him again, I am sure I will recognize him right away. Whenever I pass by Bukchung Auntie's place, I make it my business to look carefully through the window. But I've never seen him, not even once, since that night.'

'What happened in the haunted house?' Young-sil asked importunately, patting his lap gently.

'When I entered the house, a strong odour of accumulated dust engulfed me instantly. The plaster of the walls inside had peeled off, and I could see something dangling from a rafter. The place was in chaos, I could tell, even though it was pitch black.

'I sat down on the wooden floor, quite dazed. Outside it was dark as black ink. The wind was getting stronger, and the rain poured down harder. The combined sound of the ferocious, howling wind and the furious downpour gave me an eerie feeling. On top of that, I began to hear strange, horrible creaking noises throughout the entire house. Can you imagine how terrified I was?'

Young-sil sighed deeply as she listened to his gripping story. She felt quite frightened. Speaking faster in an excited tone, he continued.

22

'The place chilled me. It was the perfect time and place for a ghost to walk, and I sat there quietly waiting for the ghost to appear. But, as the rain subsided, I became so sleepy that I couldn't keep my eyes open. Finally, I must have dozed off. Then I was harshly awakened by someone grabbing my neck. Someone very strong was trying to strangle me!

'In my younger days, you know, I was a strong, healthy fighter. However, I have to admit, this man was the toughest I have ever confronted. I knew right away the man was a lot stronger than I, but I was determined to fight him. I didn't want to give in. So I fought him with all my might. Finally, I managed to knock him over. He got up swiftly from the floor. The man appeared to be easily seven feet tall. I couldn't make out his features. I couldn't recognize anything about him. I wrestled and tumbled with that giant all night. Whenever I was underneath him, he tried to strangle me. My goodness, he was strong! I don't know how long we fought. Anyway, the man finally seemed to be exhausted and came under my control. I couldn't let this golden opportunity slip. Quickly I took out a small, ornamental knife from my inner pocket and stabbed him in the heart, sitting on his stomach. I saw his face drenched with heavy sweat; when I saw him writhing in pain, I fainted.'

The maid brought in fresh tea for the storyteller and his listeners, and ginger tea for Sung-aah's grandmother. The old man drank up his hot tea with pleasure.

'What happened after that, sir?'

'Oh, that's all. That's the end of my story, my girl.'

'What happened to your knife then?'

At Young-sil's question, the old man put his tea cup down and tilted his body slightly as before. His eyes were soft as he gazed at the children.

'When I woke up next morning,' the old man explained, 'I found the knife lying near a worn-out broom at the corner of the courtyard.'

No one knew what to say to this statement.

'I vaguely recall that I threw the giant out into the courtyard, but I couldn't swear to it. I went to sleep in a room at the other end of the house. I don't even remember when or how I came to the room where I fought with the giant.'

'I understand your present house was built on the same spot where the haunted house used to be,' remarked Sung-aah's grandmother.

'That's right,' he agreed cheerfully. 'My son built it all by himself.'

The old man's son was a carpenter, and had helped build Sung-aah's father's clinic in town.

'You haven't had any more experiences with ghosts in your home?' Young-sil asked.

'No, not one.'

'I believe the house was haunted by evil spirits,' Sung-aah's grandmother stated philosophically. 'I believe the devil was testing you to find out how strong you were.'

The old man was speechless.

'I think you were very strong then,' Sung-aah's grandmothr said gently.

'Yes, ma'am, I certainly was.'

Sung-aah's mother opened the door quietly and asked the old man to stay to dinner. The old man got up half way and asked Sung-aah's grandmother:

'Are you going to join me, ma'am?'

'Oh, no, I have already had mine, thank you,' she replied politely. 'My son is having his dinner late tonight. I think he had to see his patients until now. Anyway, please go ahead and join my son across the main floor.'

'Thank you very much, ma'am. I will see you later then.' The old man left the room immediately as if he were glad to be invited. The room was brightly lit now. The light bulb and its shade glowed softly like pearls. In this place, Young-sil felt quite content. She adored her friend's house and its easy atmosphere so very different from her own. Here there was no trace of discord, anger, unpleasantness or anxiety. The house was permeated with friendliness and happiness. She especially liked the old man's tales which had brought joy and yearning for the past.

The restlessness she had experienced before she came to see her friend had vanished completely. Now Young-sil felt completely at ease. In a relaxed mood, she planned what she would do when she returned home – she would review the lessons that she had learned that day at school and then go to sleep by the fireplace. She hoped the fireplace would still be warm for her by the time she got home.

'Grandmother, please show us your ornamental knife,' Sung-aah begged.

'What do you need to see that for, my child? You may cut yourself.'

'I just want to see it,' Sung-aah insisted gently. 'You don't need to take it out of its sheath. Please, grandmother.' At her plea, her grandmother lifted her long skirt and undergarments. She untied a small sheathed ornamental knife from a cord and handed it carefully to her granddaughter.

The silver knife was handsome with its blade curved upward rather like the toe of a woman's traditional shoe. It was worth admiring. The handle was elegantly trimmed with gold and engraved with floral patterns.

'Grandmother, do yu think it was a knife like this that Koo-bae's grandfather used to stab the giant?' Sung-aah asked inocently.

'Of course not,' Young-sil put in indignantly. 'Knives most seamen use are dark-coloured and very sharp. He couldn't have used a delicate silver knife like this to hurt the giant.'

To Young-sil's mind, the old man was her idea of a seaman in every sense, a seaman who had earned his living from the sea.

When Young-sil reluctantly decided it was time to leave, her friend began to play the organ, and she was captivated by the magic power of Sung-aah's delightful music. The organ was large but worn-out. A Chinese war refugee had sold it before he returned to his home in Nanking. The organ changed hands many times until it finally found a permanent home at Sung-aah's house. Its deep soft tone touched the centre of Young-sil's heart, leaving her with a tingling feeling. The school organ in the auditorium was manual and quite a few of its keys were missing. It produced notes only when its pedals were manipulated, and its tone was loud and harsh. Unlike the school organ, Sung-aah's was operated by electricity.

Although Sung-aah barely touched the keys, Young-sil was profoundly impressed by its delicate sound. Hardly daring to breath, she timidly pressed one of the smooth white keys with her index finger. Although Young-sil was usually hasty and careless, she was extremely cautious with Sung-aah's organ. To her amazement, one single key produced a sound – a mysteriously beautiful and unearthly sound. Completely lost in her reverie of beautiful music, Young-sil listened with all her soul until it penetrated to the depth of her heart and slowly spread throughout her being, leaving the lingering effect of a hymn.

Finally Young-sil got up reluctantly to leave her friend's cosy home. The night had deepened when she went outside. Slowly she descended the hilly road and then climbed another hill in the direction of her house. All the time she was walking, Young-sil was preoccupied with the wonderful music of the organ and thinking how marvellous it would be to have an organ.

The top of her rubber shoe, which she had temporarily fixed with needle and thread, burst open as she kicked a stone. The damaged shoe was the least of her concerns; her mind was totally obsessed with the organ music. But as the shoe was hampering her progress, she took it off and the other shoe as well, and clutched them to her chest.

Barefooted, Young-sil contined on her way home, muttering softly to herself, 'What a beautiful sound the organ makes! It is a wonderful sound, indeed!'

4

Young-sil's father usually stayed in his room all day long. Sometimes he came out and walked round the courtyard. Because he was unemployed other members of the family had to work to keep up with expenses. Young-sil's mother and sister were busy sewing. They had built a small fire in a tiny iron pot for an iron. They sewed diligently, spreading the fine, delicate fabric on a worn, thin reed mat. As if she were working with quilting cotton Sinn-sil's head was fully covered with a towel.

'Please hurry up, you two,' begged Young-sil, stamping her feet in frustration. 'I want to leave now, right away.'

Young-sil had been enjoying herself playing with a straw skipping rope with her friends on the hillside when she recalled an errand she was supposed to do for her mother. Reluctantly she had stopped playing and rushed home to do her duty, only to find that her mother was not yet ready.

Young-sil could see some unfinished traditional Korean blouses turned inside out on the floor.

'Hurry up!' Young-sil burst out suddenly. Sinn-sil tried to work faster, but her mother completely ignored Young-sil's tantrum.

'I wonder if the "woman from Woonchun" is good at ironing?' Young-sil's mother mused aloud. 'Let me have those, dear. I'd better iron them for her. To be on the safe side, you know.'

Young-sil stepped onto the reed mat with her muddy feet and began to wrap the blouses in a cloth.

'What do you think you're doing, girl?' her mother grumbled. She snatched the cloth from her daughter, took out the blouses and started to press them one by one.

'Good grief!' Young-sil exclaimed scornfully. 'What a fool Mr Kim must be! How is it he can't see through his lady friend's tricks? If I were him, I would have seen what sort of person she is right away.' Young-sil chuckled.

Mr Kyung-boo Kim was a secret service detective. His mistress, the 'woman from Woonchun', was not so young, yet her sewing skill was so poor that people used to talk about it. Consequently, the mistress used to ask people to sew for her. Whenever she asked such a favour of Young-sil's mother, she would implicitly acknowledge her own shortcoming, saying, 'You don't need to attach the collar or tie fastening to my blouse, my friend. I can do that myself, you know. That's the least I can do to lighten your load.'

The 'woman from Woonchun' was only too pleased to have her blouse returned with the collar or string loose as she had requested. She never failed to choose the right time before her man came home to sew the collar and string in his presence, hoping to give him a good impression.

'Guess what I did today, my dear? I spent all day sewing this blouse,' she would tell him impressively. 'Don't you think I did a good job placing this collar nicely?'

'You shouldn't have done that, my dear,' her lover, Mr Kim Kyung-boo, would reply in an easy manner. 'Why don't you ask someone to sew for you?'

Mr Kim was short and stout. His hands and feet were small and stubby.

'I can't wear clothes sewn by others, my dear,' his mistress

27

would lie. 'I just don't feel right asking people to do something for me that I can easily do myself.'

This conversation between Mr Kim and his mistress about her sewing had been spread into evey corner of town by someone who overheard them. Now there was no one, not even the children, who was unaware of her trick. It was the woman next door who told Young-sil's mother about the rumour and how the 'woman from Woonchun' lied to her lover about her sewing skill. Young-sil's mother merely smiled at the gossip; however, Young-sil couldn't help bursting into hearty laughter, clapping her hands.

'You'd better stop that nonsense, girl,' her father roared. 'Stop it at once!' Young-sil quickly controlled herself. The tone of her father's voice was as sharp as the edge of a knife.

'Let me have the package, Mother,' Young-sil asked impatiently. 'I'd better take it before Mr Kim comes home. If I am late, she won't be able to impress him with her lies again. You know what I mean. What a fake she is!' Young-sil felt angry at her mother's slowness. Her mother got up after folding all the blouses carefully. Then she took out a suit of traditional Korean men's clothes from the dresser.

'What are those?' Young-sil asked irritably. 'Do I have to take them, too?'

'Yes, dear.'

At her mother's answer, Young-sil resigned herself to waiting and sat down on the mat, folding her legs. But she was not silent for long.

'Mum, do you remember last year when Mr Kim's child died?' Young-sil asked offhand. 'The child that was born to that Korean geisha that Mr Kim was having an affair with?'

'Yes, I do remember that, my child,' her mother replied guardedly.

'I've been thinking, Mother,' Young-sil continued excitedly, 'and I've come to the conclusion that Mr Kim's child was kidnapped by a leper. And you know what? I'm positive his present mistress was responsible. I believe the "woman from Woonchun" made an arrangement with a certain leper to kidnap Mr Kim's child. I know what I'm talking about, Mother.'

'Hush, child. What nonsense are you talking? Don't say such things again. Don't you ever say such a thing to anybody, do you hear?'

Young-sil took no notice. 'Mum, you know what I heard? Mr Kim's mistress is sterile! And I heard she takes Chinese medicine, hoping to get pregnant. But even Chinese medicine is useless in her case. Anyway, that's why she got rid of Mr Kim's child that was born to the Korean geisha. She had it kidnapped by the leper, I'm positive, Mum. I just know it was her foul play. I tell you she arranged the whole thing so that the leper would have its liver and abandon the child on the mountain!'

'Be quiet, girl! It is not true. It is a groundless rumour. Let me tell you something, my child. Once some members of the Patriotic Party attempted to go into exile in the southeastern part of Manchuria in China so that they could pursue the independence movement. Anyway, the Korean patriots took refuge in the mountain here in our village. The Japanese secret police and military police completely surrounded the mountain in order to arrest the Korean patriots. The Japanese police covered the while mountain area, and they didn't find any lepers there. Not a single one. So you see, my girl, there is no leper, and you are talking nonsense!'

'I don't care what you say, mother,' Young-sil insisted. 'I tell you the leper kidnapped Mr Kim's child according to the instruction of Mr Kim's mistress, and . . .'

'Don't be so silly, child,' her mother gave her a sharp slap on the back, finally raised to anger. 'You know it isn't true. Now control yourself and deliver these clothes to that woman right away.'

'I do remember seeing some men in bloodstained white clothing being dragged away by the Japanese military police. They all had beards that were bushy and untrimmed, and their hands were tied tightly.' Young-sil had the last word as usual.

Young-sil went out on to the courtyard, dragging her worn-out rubber shoes. She went to the pile of pine needles in the corner of the yard and cautiously took out a round cake of overcooked millet rice, which was well hidden inside the pile of pine needles. Such snacks appealed to her appetite. She took a good bite, smiling in satisfaction. Although no one else competed with her for food, at home. Young-sil had a habit of hiding such snacks anywhere she felt they would be safe.

Chewing the delicious rice cake, Young-sil walked slowly along, carrying the cloth wrapper in her arms. She could vaguely see the children playing with the skipping rope over the hill. Their high-pitched tone of harmonious chanting – one, two, three, four – mingled with the sigh of the passing wind. Oddly enough, she was not drawn by the joyous squeals. She did not feel like joining in the game anymore.

Generally speaking, Young-sil was well-adjusted to her circumstances and life style. She was accustomed to accepting her situation; consequently, she tried to make the most of any opportunity and had trained herself to appreciate little things, that added interest to her life.

Young-sil walked along the dark and chilly road, eating her millet rice cake eagerly and holding the cloth wrapper tightly in her arms. Deliberately she walked slowly, arching her back. At the entrance to the marketplace began the wide, nearly deserted road that led directly to the middle school. Mr Kim's mistress, the 'woman from Woonchun' lived on the same hill at the top of which the old man, the storyteller, also lived.

Mr Kim's mistress had a round face; and a shiny gold tooth showed whenever she smiled or opened her mouth. Her complexion was always pale, and she smoked like a man. Most people found it difficult to like her. The story about her having lived in Manchuria seemed unlikely. Young-sil could not believe Mr Kim's mistress had actually lived there as she claimed. In Young-sil's mind, Manchuria was an exotic, symbolic place where Korean patriots, fighting for independence from the Japanese oppression, made their headquarters. The name 'Manchuria' was also associated in her mind with opium addicts, prostitutes, or others involved in vice. Young-sil could not see an ordinary, dull woman like Mr Kim's mistress fitting into such a scene.

Mr Kim's mistress had narrow slit eyes like the eyes of a phoenix. They were always alert and shining, reflecting her keen common sense and her ability to handle any occurrence coolly. Although her coaxing, suggestive tone of voice indicated caprice, it could also suggest patience and compassion.

She often used to treat. Young-sil to chocolates or other kinds of sweets or biscuits. Besides her generosity, she provided Young-sil's family with valuable work by giving them sewing to do for her, which Young-sil was well aware was vital to their livelihood. When it came to the practicalities of life, Young-sil was a realist. She was grateful to Mr Kim's mistress for giving them an opportunity to earn their living. Even the sight of her dry, round face made her feel close to the woman.

Young-sil halted in front of the Japanese-style entrance as she reached Mr Kim's house, and called cheerfully, 'Hello, is anyone home?' There was no response from inside. Patiently Young-sil waited for someone to come, calling out 'hello' as loudly as she could. After a while someone opened a sliding door by the hall and Mr Kim appeared. He was wearing a pair of black-rimmed spectacles. His face was round and plump like the rest of his body and he had a very fresh healthy complexion. He was wearing traditional Korean dress, including a jacket that Young-sil had brought to him not long ago. His hands were tucked inside the cuffs of his shirt. He cast a quizzical glance towards Young-sil and beamed at her.

Mr Kim was called the 'immaculate detective' by the Japanese people who respected him for his work. He was a hero to them. Mr Kim was very proud of his job which required him to arrest any Koreans who resisted Japanese authority. He took pride in his duty to arrest, torture, even kill his fellow Koreans to enhance his own fame and power. Whenever he happened to sit with geishas, Japanese or Korean, in fancy restaurants, Mr Kim would go out of his way to brag about his cold-blooded job.

Young-sil looked up at him in awe and fear. His big eyes were blinking rapidly behind his thick-rimmed glasses.

One incident concerning him again sprang vividly to her mind, the time when her friend Soon-ock's brother, who had settled in Manchuria for a while, returned home. Somehow his secret homecoming was revealed and Mr Kim and his men were waiting for him. They arrested Soon-ock's brother at the railway station and took him to the police station for further questioning. Realizing her son's inevitable plight, Soon-ock's mother wailed hysterically as her handcuffed son was taken away by Mr Kim's men.

Young-sil could not forget this tragic scene involving her friend's family, for which Mr Kim was responsible. Young-sil could almost imagine the smell of blood still clung to his hands, and instinctively she shuddered.

'Who are you looking for?' Mr Kim asked. At his question, Young-sil flinched. His voice was high-pitched, almost metallic in nature. Even though his question was harmless and his tone kind, Young-sil could not help feeling afraid of him. She was remembering guiltily all the times she had spoken ill of Mr Kim and his mistress. She had spread the rumour that Mr Kim's mistress had arranged a secret meeting with the leper so that Mr Kim's illegitimate child could be kidnapped and eventually killed. Young-sil had also called Mr Kim a fool. Now his stare seemed to hint that he had known all along what Young-sil had been saying about his mistress and himself.

'What have you got in your arms?' Mr Kim asked in a more peremptory tone.

'Oh, this!' Young-sil began to stutter. 'It's nothing but . . .'

Suddenly Mr Kim's eyes began to flash, with impatience. Strangely, though, Young-sil became calm. This short, stout, middle-aged man did not intimidate her any more.

She smiled at him as she tried to work out how she could avoid answering his question without offending him. For she realized she could not tell him the truth about the contents of the package. She did not want to embarrass his mistress. She solved her dilemma by replying politely, 'I'm looking for Kuy-dong's mother, sir'.

'Oh, the maid, I see!' This time Mr Kim looked at Young-sil with interest. In his eyes, Young-sil was full of vigour and her expression was bright. Even though she was not pretty, her face was interesting.

As they were engaged in conversation, Mr Kim's mistress appeared in the room facing the courtyard. Unlike most days, Mr Kim's mistress looked tidy and well-groomed today. She was wearing a clean apron over her long skirt. Usually her hair was ill-kept and untidy, as if she had just woken up; but today she was very presentable.

Young-sil presumed she made an effort to please Mr Kim whenever he was around the house. When she saw Young-sil with the cloth wrapper in her arms, Mr Kim's mistress became very embarrassed.

'What brings you here?' she asked quietly, going to Young-sil quickly.

'I was sent for by Kuy-dong's mum,' Young-sil replied, twisting her entire body. 'I haven't the faintest idea what this is. I was just told to deliver this package to your maid, that's all!'

'Is that right?' Mr Kim's mistress replied, snatching the wrapper. 'Let me have it then!'

Although Young-sil knew that she ought to receive money from Mr Kim's mistress for her mother's work, she decided to come back another time. Her common sense told her it would be better to make another trip than to risk embarrassing Mr Kim's mistress by exposing her secret.

'Why don't you come back the day after tomorrow?' Mr Kim's mistress suggested meaningly. 'You can take some rice cakes back to Kuy-dong's family then.'

'Yes, ma'am, I'll certainly return then.' Young-sil and Mr Kim's mistress understood each other; they had tacitly reached an agreement.

As her own name was mentioned, the maid, old and frail, slowly poked her head out of the kitchen. Mr Kim's mistress almost pushed the maid back into the kitchen and disappeared quickly inside.

Young-sil turned to leave the house and sent a broad, friendly smile to Mr Kim, who had been watching his mistress and Young-sil.

'Take care, sir,' Young-sil bade him farewell. Mr Kim did not acknowledge her presence in any way.

'Don't you ride horseback while you're on duty, sir?' Young-sil asked ingenuously. 'I'm sure I've seen you on a horse a few times on my way to school.'

Mr Kim gave a gasp of surprise at her question and looked at her with new interest as if he were well pleased.

'Is your horse very expensive?' she asked again. Mr Kim burst into hearty laughter.

'I was told your police horse was brought from Manchuria when his master, a mounted bandit, was captured. Is it true that the horse came all the way from Manchuria, sir?'

'Please don't make me laugh, girl,' Mr Kim said, still laughing.

From the other side of the house, Mr Kim's mistress cast a suspicious glance towards Young-sil and Mr Kim. Bending her head low, Young-sil bowed to them, still smiling broadly.

*   *   *

A couple of days later, Young-sil stopped by Mr Kim's house to get the money on her way home from school. Mr Kim's mistress came out to the entrance hall right away and paid her willingly as Young-sil had expected.

'Here it is,' Mr Kim's mistress handed her the money. 'This is for your mother, and this is for yourself.'

Mr Kim's mistress put an extra, crisp Won in her hand. Since Young-sil's mother charged only half a Won per blouse, Young-sil realized that the extra Won was equal to the fee of two blouses. She was exceedingly happy with this unexpected bonus.

'Would you like to take some rice cakes home?' Mr Kim's mistress asked feebly and went inside hurriedly. She looked unhappy as if something were troubling her, yet even in her confusion she did not forget that she had said the other day that she would give some rice cakes to Young-sil and her family.

A mixed aroma of frying and steaming food emanated from the kitchen, tantalizing Young-sil's appetite. Sniffing the delightful aroma, Young-sil congratulated herself on her luck in receiving the extra Won.

Mr Kim's mistress came out with a package wrapped in white paper and handed it to Young-sil. She gazed at Young-sil thoughtfully.

'Are you busy today?' she asked slowly. She spoke as if in a dream or deep thought. Young-sil shook her head emphatically in the negative. She was not at all busy, in fact.

'That's good, then,' Mr Kim's mistress said with determination. 'Why don't you take this food to your house and come right back? Today is Mr Kim's birthday, you see. I need you to do some errands for me when the guests arrive. Will you?'

Before Mr Kim's mistress had finished her sentence, Young-sil was halfway through the hall doorway.

'I'll be right back,' Young-sil emphasized. 'I'll be here before you know it.' She dashed out to the street, breathing heavily. As soon as she reached home, Young-sil cleaned herself up with extra care. She washed her dust-covered feet carefully and brushed her hair back and moistened it with water. Then she reappeared at Mr Kim's house, her hair decorated with a pink plastic pin, patterned with cherry blossom.

This time Mr Kim's mistress greeted Young-sil with a lively expression. She looked much happier than before. Several women were in the kitchen, preparing food for Mr Kim's birthday party.

The master bedroom was furnished with a fancy folding screen, and handsome cushions were laid here and there. Colourful patterns on the cotton cushions and pictures of peony blossoms and beautiful pheasants on the folding screen enchanted Young-sil. To her disappointment, however, Mr Kim's mistress took her to a small, shabby room in a secluded wing of the house, adjacent to the store room. Young-sil could see a large pair of women's rubber shoes on the floor near the door. The worn-out shoes were covered with mud.

'Will you stay with this woman and keep her company?' Mr Kim's mistress asked in a lower tone. 'Please offer her some fruit. Later on, I'll send a nice supper in to you. You must stay with her all the time. You mustn't let her out of your sight. Specifically, she can't come out while the party's going on. Do you understand?' Having made quite sure Young-sil understood her wishes, Mr Kim's mistress disappeared into the main living quarters. Young-sil could hear people arriving for the birthday party and calling to Mr Kim from outside. She opened the door and looked into the unlit room. A middle-aged woman was sitting there all alone. The woman was wearing a long, light-coloured cotton skirt and an unseasonable Chinese silk blouse that reflected light in the darkness. The woman had broad shoulders and deep wrinkles furrowed her round face. She appeared to be under great strain. As Young-sil sat down near her, the woman glanced at her without interest and then faced the wall again. Time passed slowly, but the woman kept her face turned to the wall, and continued to maintain the same posture. Young-sil's active mind dwelt on the exciting activities in the main living quarters; however, she realized she was under obligation to watch her woman.

Different kinds of rice cakes and some peeled, discoloured, bite-size pieces of apple were on a small plate in front of the woman. Young-sil gazed at her attentively, wondering who she was. Hungrily, Young-sil sampled a few rice cakes and scrutinized the woman's face with interest. The woman continued to stare at the wall, ignoring Young-sil. Her distant gaze was dream-like, as if she were looking at some faraway place; in fact, she did not appear to be looking at anything at

35

all. In contrast with her blank gaze, the muscles round her mouth and cheeks were so tense and tight that she appeared to be on the verge of a convulsion.

Observing the woman's facial expression, Young-sil realized that the woman was fighting to control a deeper sense of despair and sorrow than Young-sil could comprehend. The woman's desperate silence also suggested a brooding anger as she sat immobile like a stone statue of Buddha.

'Please, ma'am, have some of these,' Young-sil offered kindly, pushing the plate of cakes closer to her side. Young-sil wanted to be kind to the woman; she wanted to console this sorrow-stricken creature, not just because she had been asked to watch her by Mr Kim's mistress. Somehow the woman's unspoken sadness had touched Young-sil; she could feel an enormous sense of sadness spreading in her own heart. Even though she did not have even the vaguest idea what kind of sad story surrounded this woman, Young-sil felt that she understood somehow. She felt for this wretched woman a spontaneous compassion that sprang from the bottom of her heart.

'Please, ma'am, try this,' Young-sil offered again.

As if affected by Young-sil's imploring tone, the woman shifted her gaze from the wall and looked at Young-sil silently.

'Who are you?' she asked feebly. Without waiting for Young-sil's reply, the woman suddenly began sobbing.

'How can you ask me to eat? How can anyone expect me to eat?' The woman began to sob violently. She was choked with tears. Young-sil's eyes were dimmed with tears of her own.

'Please don't cry, ma'am. Please don't.'

'I can't help it. How can I?' the woman wailed in a shrill, unpleasant voice. At her wailing someone rushed to the room from across the courtyard, halted in front momentarily, and then retreated. Suddenly Young-sil came to her senses, remembering that Mr Kim's birthday party was going on in the main wing of the house. Recalled to her duty, she spoke sharply to the woman.

'Compose yourself!' Young-sil ordered her. The woman stopped crying obediently, stuffing a piece of cloth into her mouth to control her sobs.

'Please don't cry, ma'am,' said Young-sil, speaking more softly this time. 'Listen to me, please. I'll tell you something,'

Young-sil rubbed the woman's back gently. Abruptly, the woman lifted her head.

'What kind of child are you? Who are you, anyway?' the woman asked curiously.

'Me? I'm nobody. I am not related to anyone in this household.'

The woman held the piece of cloth to her eyes to control her tears.

'Where are you from, ma'am?' Since her tone of voice – compassionate and understanding – won the woman's trust, she finally opened up to her young companion after a short silence.

As the woman's sad, stunning story was finally revealed, Young-sil and the woman wept together. The woman was Mr Kim's wife. In tears, she told Young-sil of her hard lot, and Young-sil, also in tears, listened to the story sympathetically. They were still weeping quietly together when suddenly, violent footsteps were heard approaching the room. The door was flung open and Mr Kim's outraged figure appeared. The woman and Young-sil started up instantly at this sudden and intimidating apparition.

Mr Kim had never dreamed his lawful wife would show up on his birthday to confront his mistress. In his rage, Mr Kim grabbed his wife by the collar and dragged her brutally out into the street.

The following day the whole town had become aware of the embarrassing incident at Mr Kim's house. Since Mrs Kim had never before dared to confront her husband's mistresses openly, her attempt to compete with the present mistress was shocking news to the villagers.

Never before had Mrs Kim showed resentment or jealousy toward the mistress. She had been generally considered to be a helpless, and even stupid woman for whom most people felt sorry. Mr Kim was notorious for his brutality; people called him 'stinking swine' because he was so cold-blooded. Everyone agreed that Mr Kim was hopelessly cruel and that his treatment of his lawful wife was unfair and unjust. People despised his vulgar behaviour, dashing out that night in his bare feet, leaving his guests in the room, to beat his wife. Yet in spite of her husband's shameful reputation, Mrs Kim's clumsy attempt to deal with the mistress made her the focus of gossip and mockery. People could not believe the way Mrs Kim had made a fool of herself by appearing on her husband's birthday. Even though they criticized Mr Kim's savageness, most village people could not help sneering at his wife, who was foolish enough to try to compete with a woman like her husband's present mistress. The outcome of the contest between Mrs Kim and the mistress was already decided.

Before Mr Kim established his position in the world, his wife used to sell potatoes house to house, in her bare feet, carrying a large wooden bowl on her head. However, after his success, Mr Kim turned a cold shoulder to his faithful wife, neglecting her for one concubine after another. His present mistress, the 'woman from Woonchun', took Mrs Kim's place, enjoying an easy life.

Even though her heart had been swollen for so long with every manner of hurt and humiliation, Mrs Kim's recent behaviour was regarded as absurd instead of understandable. That morning she had come in through the back door and stood motionless in front of the kitchen door. The women in the kitchen noticed her but did not pay much attention. Her blouse of Chinese silk indicated that she could not be a beggar, so they looked up at her in curiosity, and were amazed to see who she was.

'Aren't your Haak-soo's mother? Don't you live on Sinnheung-dong?' one of the women asked. They couldn't help showing their surprise.

The illegitimate child who had been born to Mr Kim and his Korean geisha and had died the previous year had been named Haak-soo. Even though the child had not been brought up by Mrs Kim, she was generally called 'Haak-soo's mother' by the village women.

'It's Haak-soo's mother who lives in Sinnheung-dong!' one woman finally whispered to Mr Kim's mistress, who had been too busy to notice Mrs Kim's sudden appearance in her house. Several women stepped down into the courtyard, hoping to persuade Mrs Kim to leave. Mrs Kim made not the slightest movement whatsoever in response to their friendly request.

In great astonishment and embarrassment, Mr Kim's mistress took Mrs Kim to the room in the outer wing of the house, addressing her with respect as 'elder sister'. Indeed, Mr Kim's mistress had no choice but to treat Mrs Kim respectfully, since she realized that guests would be arriving any minute and had no wish to have an unpleasant confrontation with Mrs Kim if she could prevent it. In fact she was even willing to make a ceremonial bow to Mrs Kim after the birthday party if Mr Kim would permit it.

Nobody knew how Mr Kim learned of his wife's presence, but as soon as he found out, he created a disgraceful scene, treating his wife harshly and shamefully. People talked about it as freely as if they had witnessed the whole thing with their own eyes; how Mrs Kim, had been led to a room in an outer wing, and had remained silent, sitting by a dining table until she was dragged out by her husband. It was true that Mrs Kim had spoken to no one since she arrived. Out of curiosity several women, one by one, attempted to speak to Mrs Kim but each was ignored. Even Mr Kim's mistress, who had addressed Mrs Kim with respect, was completely ignored. Mrs Kim trembled uncontrollably with indescribable chagrin and resentment towards her treacherous husband and his mistress. Young-sil was the only soul with whom Mrs Kim conversed candidly. Mr Kim behaved like a mad dog as if he would do violence his wife. After these traumatic events, Young-sil felt numb; it had all happened too fast for her to take in, even though her own head had been banged against the wall as a result of Mr Kim's lunatic pushing.

After Mr Kim finally returned to his guests, his mistress came to see Young-sil.

'I'm sorry about everything, dear,' she consoled Young-sil without looking at her. 'I'm grateful for your efforts. You've done very well.' All in all, Young-sil felt she had acquitted herself well. She congratulated herself on fulfilling her responsibility to keep Mrs Kim in the room.

'This is not very much,' Mr Kim's mistress handed Young-sil some money timidly. 'Please do not tell anyone what has happened tonight.'

Young-sil lifted her long skirt and carefully put the folded money into the pocket in her bloomers. Just as she was about to leave by the front gate, Young-sil hastily returned to the room. She had remembered something. The rice cakes and fruit were scattered throughout the room, badly crushed by Mr Kim's kicking and stamping. Calmly Young-sil gathered these up and put them into her skirt.

39

On the edge of sadness, she walked slowly away. She sighed deeply at the turmoil of life's confusion. She felt touched by the tragedy in the depths of her young heart.

*   *   *

It did not take very long for Mrs Kim to resume her peddling after the shameful incident at Mr Kim's house. One day at the end of April, when it was still cold and dreary, Young-sil went to the country looking for wild garlic. Wild garlic could be found about five miles away from the village, near the Soo-sung Bridge, which was made of steel and built over a stream flowing through a sandy field. Usually hard to find, wild garlic could very occasionally be found in deep soil. The chilly wind over the open field lifted the sand off the ground and chapped the fingers of the girls as they hunted for wild garlic around the bridge. Their plump faces and tiny hands that held small picks felt the bite of both wind and sand.

It was getting colder and Young-sil was hungry. Although she had a long way to walk home, Young-sil did not want to give up her expectation of finding the rare wild garlic. So she eagerly dug and poked around for the bulbs, which were as delicate as threads of silk. She was thrilled by each bulb of fresh wild garlic she dug up. The texture of the skin covering its round shape and its cream colour were very pleasing to her. Her enthusiasm in digging up more and more garlic was so intense that Young-sil had completely forgotten the temperature. She was so carried away that she was quite oblivious of the gathering chill, unlike her shivering friends.

A train raced by over the steel bridge. Its great vibration seemed to shake the entire plain, and tiny clouds seemed to move more rapidly.

'Hey, look at this!' Young-sil showed off the biggest bulb of garlic, pulling it out by its silk from the basket. 'This colour is just like that of a lampshade. You know, those round, creamy shades in Japanese houses.' Her friend remained mute, paying no attention to Young-sil's remark. Her pink poplin skirt fluttered in the wind. Young-sil and her friends walked all the way back to the small railway station. As they looked back to the steel bridge, it seemed tiny and insignificant in the distance.

The station had no building or other facilities whatsoever. Only a barbed wire fence identified it as the location of a train depôt. A few women peddlers crouched on the white sandy ground around the station, waiting for the next train to board. They put their worn-out rubber shoes on top of the fishy-smelling empty sacks in their large scooped wooden bowls. Their faces looked rough and coarse, beaten by the strong wind from the sea. They gazed expressionlessly in the direction from which the next train would appear. Young-sil easily recognized a familiar face among them.

'Please, ma'am,' Young-sil called to her with great joy and excitement. 'You live at Sinneheung-dong, don't you?' Mrs Kim turned to look at her. Seeing Young-sil's beaming face, she turned her head in the other direction, facing her peddler friends. Her expression was blank, emotionless as if she had already forgotten her little friend. Her stony face strongly suggested that she had no feelings left for anyone or anything even if she did still remember her encounter with Young-sil at her husband's birthday party. Mrs Kim appeared to be absolutely numb as if she were abandoned to despair. The women peddlers took out greasy pouches from their skirt belts, and Mrs Kim did the same. The women counted their money carefully, all looking very serious as they were about to determine their profits for the day.

Pale sunrays played hide-and-seek, showering down the light whenever the wind lifted the veil of the scattered clouds.

5

The mild weather continued, reminding Young-sil to attend Sunday school at church. She knew it was almost time for her church's annual revival service on the mountain ridge. The annual rivival was followed by a picnic or a big garden party which usually drew a huge crowd. The service was held on the same mountain ridge overlooking the brothel quarter.

In order to reach the mountain ridge, the worshippers had to pass through the street of brothels. This meant that they could not sing hymns while passing through this notorious street. Church people had been battling with this problem for some time now, and each year they sent a petition to the city authorities to grant them permission to make a detour through the thickly wooded shrine area.

When Young-sil began attending church regularly, she found other young people bursting with excitement about the approaching revival service on the mountain ridge. The church youth group leader, Mr Chang, humbly promised that they would be able to attend the revival by the 'grace of God'.

Mr Chang's father ran a small restaurant which specialized in noodles, and hot steam from the restaurant spread into the street and immediately evaporated into the atmosphere.

Mr Chang wore gold-rimmed spectacles which looked like ladies' glasses. It was not just his glasses which gave him a feminine appearance; everything he possessed was dainty and feminine for a man of his age. Take his pointed shoes and exceptionally bright blue suit for instance; his mode of attire alone made him seem effeminate. Mr Chang lived with his father at the restaurant where they shared a room. The restaurant had only one entrance; consequently, Mr Chang had no choice but to use the front door. He would tiptoe across the mud in front of the restaurant and come outside. As soon as he reached the dry ground just outside the door, he would wipe the points of his shoes with his clean white handkerchief.

Although Mr Chang had attended one of the best universities in Japan for seven years, he had not yet graduated. Since his father, Deacon Chang, had firmly decided not to spend another Won on his son's education, there was no immediate prospect of Mr Chang's returning to Japan to continue his education. However, he had not entirely given up hope of resuming his studies.

Now Young-sil attended church on a regular basis; she even used to go to Wednesday and Friday evening services, although she often found the Bible stories and long prayers tedious and tiring. Whenever she became bored with the devotions, she used to make some kind of excuse and go outside to pace back and forth.

The wooden church with its slate roof was very old; it was situated on its own, away from the village, on the slope of the hill. A parsonage and a bell tower, also with a slate roof, stood side by side next to the church. The church on the hill looked down along the cement breakwater which ran between a small field and a local bus route. From the hill there was an excellent view of the vast sea in the distance. Young-sil gazed out over the sea, standing by the edge of the cliff, where there was no rail or fence to protect her from falling.

Surprisingly, the harbour people were not interested in the sea. Except for those who earned their living directly from the ocean, most people rarely went near it or bothered to watch the coast without an ulterior reason. Young-sil, however, was filled with love for the sea. She found it fascinating just to watch the vast, rolling waves in the distance. She especially loved to observe the changing moods of the sea. To her it wore different expressions according to the weather – different moods on sunny, cloudy, calm, and windy days.

Today was sunny and bright and the morning sea glistened where the sun's rays touched it. The horizon, where sea and sky met, was a clear blue just like the sky on a perfectly clear morning. Gentle wavelets danced in splendid succession, reflecting the sunlight. Reluctantly, Young-sil turned away from her view of the sea and began to walk towards the parsonage. It was almost time for Sunday school to be over. She could see adult worshippers climbing the hill to gather for the service. Church also served as a place to exchange conversation and gossip among the villagers. The main topic of conversation at present was the second wife of a rich but bedridden elderly man who had been seriously ill for some time. He was partially paralysed from a stroke and had lost the function of speech. The wife always came to church early and left before the service ended. Since she had no children, she was seriously worried about what was to become of her after her husband's death. Unless he had guaranteed that she would benefit under his will, his young wife would be faced with severe poverty. Consequently, she was always anxious and looked desperately troubled.

Besides this worried woman, there were a mentally retarded young woman, a barber's mute son, and the mother of the schoolboy Kyung-sik Yoon. These were the main subjects of conversation among church members.

Kyung-sik's mother was the centre of attention. She was the one for whom people had most sympathy. She was a woman of sorrow, a classic symbol of tragedy. Her well-shaped nose

43

expressed her dignity as a proud woman; yet her roving eyes were always bloodshot, and made her look as if she were always crying. She seemed to be unsettled, always seeking something. Somehow she managed to form her mouth into an unnatural, autonomous faint smile.

Young-sil walked alongside the wooden fence beside the parsonage, watching people in their best Sunday clothes going to church. Some had hymn books under their arms; some held Bibles bound in leather. The parsonage was small and shabby with two long rooms and a small kitchen. However, it was clean and very quiet. During the summer numerous flowers decorated the entire courtyard with a splendid display of colour.

The parsonage had been built by Kyung-sik's grandfather, first minister and founder of the church. Now the sunlight penetrated into the side wooden veranda through a small crack in the sliding door. The short, stout minister smiled warmly with his eyes as he slowly walked to the church. A little boy in the courtyard, whose name was Hisaya, smiled broadly as his eyes met Young-sil's. Whenever this boy with the Japanese name smiled, his dimples showed. He had rosy cheeks and was very engaging. He was not yet old enough to go to school.

This little boy was regarded with disdain as if he were a child of the devil. Yet Hisaya was a pleasant child, always smiling and friendly. He walked towards Young-sil, hoping she would speak to him. Young-sil could detect a pleasant odour about him – the smell of milk or apples. In spite of his friendliness, he was treated as a social outcast by the village people. Hisaya's good-natured, beautiful mother, Ae-kyung, was born in Seoul and had had a good education there at Ewha Women's University. She was considered a 'modern woman'. Now, however, she was no more than a very popular, high-class prostitute in Wonjin. As a student Ae-kyung eloped to Japan with her professor, and a few years later returned to Wonjin bringing the baby Hisaya with her. Hisaya was not the son of the professor with whom she had eloped. Since she came to Wonjin with her son, most of the well-to-do and influential families in town had been affected in one way or another by Ae-kyung's destructive wand.

Her latest victim was Kyung-sik's mother, who had suffered from Ae-kyung's intervention in her life for a good many years now. Kyung-sik's father was a law student, and, as the son of the late minister, well-respected and widely admired until he met Ae-kyung. Since she stepped into his life and introduced him to strong drink, Kyung-sik's father had deserted his family for her, ignoring the world's criticisms and sneers.

Ae-kyung had never take adequate care of her son, Hisaya; in many ways he was neglected. Of course, she provided him with a comfortable life, expensive clothes and plenty of pocket money. Yet, she did not allow him to stay in the house during the day. Sometimes she refused to open the door for him, and he was forced to spend the night outside. The minister's wife, a distant relative of Ae-kyung, entreated her to reform. Ae-kyung turned totally deaf ears to her prayers and to the ceaseless sermons of the minister. Ae-kyung chose to remain a prostitute and her son, Hisaya, had been living like an orphan with the minister's family ever since.

'Are you going to Sunday school now?' Hisaya asked in a hesitant tone, fearful that Young-sil might ignore him completely.

'Yes, I am,' she replied kindly. 'What are you doing?' The little boy was relieved and delighted by her response; he ran into the house and returned with something in his arms, smiling all over his face.

'Look at this!' he pointed to the toy. 'This train runs whenever I push the button. See?' His small toy train ran on its rails, blinking tiny lights.

'My word!' Young-sil exclaimed, very much impressed. 'I have never seen a toy like this before. Let me try, please.' Young-sil pushed the button strongly so that the small toy train would run faster.

Hisaya was delighted at her interest. Since he had been told not to wander around the church grounds on Sundays, Hisaya had no one to talk to and Sundays were unbearably boring for him. Afraid that she might leave him right away, he studied her face carefully, feeling quite uneasy.

'Did your mother buy this toy for you?' she asked. Hisaya nodded his head emphatically.

'How about your nice clothes?'

'Yes, she got these for me too.'

'I envy you very much, Hisaya,' Young-sil said earnestly. 'My mother doesn't buy me even one piece of candy.'

Hisaya paused for a moment in astonishment and then gave her a wide grin. He appeared to be pleased with her candid statement. Young-sil could hear people joyfully singing a hymn in the church. Children's worship must be nearly over. Leaving Hisaya, she went to the edge of the cliff and looked down. Suddenly she saw a shadowy figure standing on the grey breakwater below. The figure was not wearing a hat and had its hands thrust into the trousers pockets. It looked like Kyung-sik. She couldn't recognize his face but she was almost certain that it was he; there was something characteristic about the set of his shoulders: something gloomy and dark, and yet something sweet as well about his features. . . .

He had not attended church, which his grandfather had founded and where his father used to take him, holding hands, to kneel down in front of the Cross of Jesus Christ.

The shadow stood facing the sea for a while and then started walking past the breakwater. He jumped from one rock to another and then disappeared behind the breakwater.

Young-sil felt momentarily a keen pain in her heart. Perplexed, she didn't know what this feeling was, but it swelled increasingly until it seemed to fill her heart.

Next moment she was climbing down the steep cliff. The upstanding rocks on the cliff were so dangerous that only a few minutes ago the Sunday school teacher had given her a stern warning not to go near them.

Young-sil was in a desperate hurry to reach the main road. She felt she could not afford to waste time by taking a safer route. She tore her skirt and scratched her legs as she climbed down, sliding occasionally and shifting her arms and shoulders in order to maintain her balance. Trying not to fall, bracing herself with her hands on the harsh soil, she bruised her hands badly, but she did not stop and finally she arrived on the flat, safe ground below. Hastily, she crossed the road and passed near the dam. As she walked closer to the bank, she could vividly hear the waves rushing to the shore. The sea that looked so calm and mild from the cliffs was now roaring like a raging lion.

Young-sil looked down the rocky beach, which was intimidating in appearance. She could see Kyung-sik lying motionless on a wide, flat rock close to the shore. His hands were clasped under his head and he was looking at the sky.

Restless waves rushed up to the rock and broke into foam and spray. The rushing water drops seemed to soak Kyung-sik's entire body as it splashed against the rock. The strong tide that flowed back and forth seemed to be trying to pull him into the sea. His puny body seemed helpless against the power of the giant waves.

Without reservation Young-sil skipped over the small dam bank and approached Kyung-sik. Still breathing heavily from running, she stopped at his side. Suddenly, she felt hot with shame. *Why am I here? What made me come to him? What did I want to tell him, anyway?* Young-sil could not answer these questions. She blamed the supernatural power that had brought her here. She felt as if she had been drawn irresistibly by some gigantic magnet. Her sense of guilt and humiliation made her angry.

Kyung-sik turned his head to see who was standing beside him. As he recognized the girl, standing there alone, he sat up halfway and looked closely at her. His stare embarrassed Young-sil very much. How she regretted coming to see him; she realized she had made an irretrievable mistake. His eyes were full of curiosity mixed with surprise at her visit. As she noticed these signs in his eyes, Young-sil was enveloped in feelings of regret and despair. She should never have come here. There was no excuse or reason for her to chase after this schoolboy.

In this mood of despair, she regretted she was so close to Kyung-sik. 'I know I am not pretty; in fact, I'm very ugly. Even my hair is coarse,' she thought. The last thing she wanted him to see was her untidy appearance.

Gradually Kyung-sik's sceptical eyes became gentle and friendly. When Young-sil noticed this change, strangely her heart sank still further and she started to run away fast, without looking back even once, farther and farther as if she were being chased. She skipped over the bank without any difficulty and soon put herself at quite a distance from Kyung-sik. As if she were riding the waves on the sea, Young-sil felt a restless uncertainty in her body. She continued to run rapidly along, her body vibrating with sensation. At a safe distance from him, she finally managed to look back.

She could see Kyung-sik still standing, with his back towards the sea and looking in her direction. 'He is looking at me, yes, no doubt about it, he is looking at *me!*' she shouted in her heart, filled with delight. Breathing heavily, somehow she could sense an intensity of feeling emanating from Kyung-sik and spreading into each cell of her body.

Chapter Two
SUMMER

1

A spiral metal ornament hung under the eaves of the Three
Star general store. The spiral had different colours – red,
green, blue and yellow – and rotated as the breeze caressed it.
As it turned, it reflected bright light from an electric lamp.
The whole area was illuminated by flashes of the coloured
reflections, giving a cool appearance.

The owner of the general store gave an immediate
impression of being a typical Japanese. It was not just the
Japanese wooden shoes he always wore. He was bald and
always wore shorts. Perhaps his long experience in dealing
with Japanese people had something to do with his appearance, causing him to resemble them. At any rate, he was
fanatically clean; he kept his store fastidiously, cleaning all day
long – dusting, sweeping and arranging. In spite of this habit,
he was easy to get along with. Because of his cheerful, easy-
going personality, the village people loved to visit him for a
chat. In front of his store he and his friends talked ceaselessly,
sitting on a wide rectangular wooden platform. The night
deepened as they engaged in easy, good-natured conversation.
Little girls played nearby with colourful glass marbles. Young-
sil sat with the adults, being entertained by their endless
gossip. Her eyes feasted on the items displayed on the table
outside the store – the shiny metal spiral rotating in the

49

breeze, sweets in the glass jar, notebooks, pencil cases, and coloured socks. Glass marbles and small toys were arranged in a small cardboard box on the ground. Young-sil was filled with rich contentment and immense happiness, even though she knew she could not afford to buy even the cheapest toy. It made her feel good just to look at all of these things and to imagine that she owned each kind of toy in the store. Unlike most children, Young-sil had learned to accept her circumstances. She was well adapted to her situation and lived accordingly. She was able to deal with daily events without complaining, and kept herself under control with no regrets or hard feelings.

'There's no doubt in my mind that Mr Choi, the fire station chief, has gone absolutely insane,' someone commented in an accent typical of Seoul. The standard Seoul accent sounded foreign in this village. The village people used only local dialects and were accustomed to other regional dialects, regarding the Seoul accent as weak and dull in comparison with other dialects. They even considered it frivolous and over-sensitive and looked down on anyone with a Seoul accent, thinking he must be a feeble person. However, in spite of this prejudice, they listened as the man continued his story in the thin, high-pitched tone of his Seoul accent.

'I had a rather awkward experience with Mr Choi today,' the man recounted. 'I was really embarrassed.'

'Why? What did he do to you?'

'Well, when he saw me on the road, Mr Choi saluted me with respect. And then he took out a bundle of name cards from his jacket pocket and began to explain them to me, one by one. I couldn't understand a word he was talking about. He was kind of mumbling to himself. I didn't think he was ever going to let me go.'

'Oh, that reminds me of the other day,' another man said excitedly. 'I saw Mr Choi standing in the middle of the road, standing still there for about fifteen minutes. I thought he might be waiting for someone.'

'I don't believe he was waiting for anyone,' the man with the Seoul accent said drily. 'Anyway, I told Mr Choi I had to go. When I asked him to excuse me, he glared at me. The way he looked at me scared the living daylights out of me.'

The listeners laughed cheerfully. The man with the Seoul

accent seemed well pleased with the favourable response he was receiving from his audience.

'The way he glared at me was so extraordinary, you see. I can't describe it. At any rate, Mr Choi suddenly said in a very low voice, "Please, listen to me carefully. I'm going to tell you something very important." His voice really frightened me.'

'What a shame you had such an upsetting time,' one of the listeners said sympathetically. 'Mr Choi has a tendency to talk to anyone he thinks important or interesting.' This candid statement made the man with the Seoul accent proud of himself. He was glad that someone regarded him as influential. He supposed a professional man like Mr Choi, the fire station chief, would not salute him unless he were worthy of respect.

As the men were engaged in conversation barefooted women carrying large wooden trays on their heads passed by. Those on the wooden platform spat contemteously as the strong odour of seaweed on the trays assailed their nostrils.

'Do you really believe Mr Choi is on the verge of going off his head?' one of them asked.

'If he is, how can he hold down his job at the fire station?'

'Well, fire doesn't break out every day, you know.'

The proprietor, who had been inside to attend to a customer, now walked towards his friends, dragging his wooden shoes.

'I think he is crazy,' he put in in a rusty tone. 'When we had that horrible fire at the sardine factory not long ago, I am sure Mr Choi nearly lost his mind.'

'If the fire chief loses his mind whenever fire breaks out,' someone commented cynically, 'he must have an extraordinary mental capacity to handle all the fires in town.'

'The fire at the factory, as you recall, was the most terrible in our town history. The oil made the fire worse. Whenever people tried to put out the fire with water, it seemed to get worse and worse. The sky of Wonjin town was blackened by smoke for three days and nights.'

'I bet Mr Choi was worried about losing his job then,' the man with the Seoul accent put in coldly. The proprietor merely smiled at this unfriendly remark.

'I don't believe he was concerned about being sacked,' he replied mildly. 'I think Mr Choi began to go off his head when he witnessed so many people being burned to death during that horrible fire.'

'Don't you think Mr Choi has been a bit crazy since he lost his wife? Perhaps being a lonely widower has been too much for him to cope with, do you reckon?'

'I don't know about that,' the proprietor replied. 'I don't pry into personal matters, you know.'

The proprietor was also widely known as 'Bong-chun's father'. His son Bong-chun, born in a town called Bongchun, was named after his birth place. It was true that the proprietor seldom talked idly to anyone. He meant what he said.

'Mr Choi has been always polite, saluting his friends,' Young-sil suddenly interrupted. 'He may be a little strange, but he is not crazy! Just because he talks funny, that doesn't mean he is insane!'

Sitting on the edge of the wooden platform, Young-sil corrected their views of Mr Choi. She had not been happy listening to people criticizing Mr Choi. As far as she was concerned, Mr Choi was a man of honour and dignity. Mr Choi wore a uniform just like a policeman's, and he always looked serious.

Whenever she met him in the street, Young-sil always greeted him warmly as 'Soon-hee's daddy'. Mr Choi usually saluted her with respect, without a trace of smile. Young-sil could not deny the fact that Mr Choi was not normal. His behaviour was often strange. She had been aware of his abnormality for some time now. However, she always remembered the loving way he treated his daughter. He was always kind and considerate to Soon-hee. Sometimes he would build a fire and talk with her with much animation. He even paid serious attention to his daughter's mindless prattling.

At Young-sil's sudden interruption the people merely stared at her, mildly shocked. Ignoring her, they immediately resumed their conversation as if nothing had happened, changing the subject, however.

'By the way, folks, Kyu-dong has had a baby,' one mentioned with pleasure.

'She hasn't! You aren't serious, are you?'

'I'm serious. She gave birth to a fine baby boy.'

'I wonder who's responsible. How in the world could anyone take advantage of a mute like her? Whoever it was, he must be a worthless creep.'

'Perhaps we can ask her who made her pregnant.'

'Even if she knows, she can't say a word, you know that,' the proprietor said, grinning.

'Time will tell, won't it? When the baby grows older, then we can identify the man.'

'If the baby takes after his mother, I don't think we stand a chance of determining who his father is.'

People freely exchanged their opinions. Then, abruptly, total silence fell on them as they saw a young woman approaching. The woman who had interrupted their busy conversation was Ae-kyung, the most notorious prostitute in town. Her short skirt and high heeled shoes showed off her well shaped legs. The little handbag she carried was another indication of her free spirit. Few women were to be seen in such modern dress in the town of Wonjin. Her hair style, its side parting, was very attractive and becoming to her. Her skin was fair; her oval-shaped face and straight nose accentuated her striking beauty. She was reminiscent of a white lily in the field.

As Ae-kyung passed by them, she cast them a quick glance. They could not accuse her of looking vulgar. In fact, there was a touch of elegance and refinement in her appearance. All in all, she was quite delightful and charming. The men could detect a subtle yet pleasant fragrance that came from her as she passed by. Even after she had entirely vanished from their sight, these men remained completely lost for words, looking still in the direction from which the sound of Ae-kyung's foosteps had faded.

In spite of her reputation as a worthless, untrustworthy whore, no one dared to utter a word against her. Not a single unkind remark was made. They did not seem even to breathe regularly. A sudden, uncomfortable air descended upon the men.

'You'd better get going home now, young lady. I bet it's past your bedtime,' the proprietor advised Young-sil. Honouring his request, she came down the wooden platform and slowly walked back home.

The sea wind blew through the alley. In the daytime the sun was strong and hot, but the night air was crisp and cool. Summer nights in Wonjin attracted no mosquitoes or moths; it was a very pleasant time of the year. The stars in the sky over Wonjin twinkled brightly through the night. Young-sil inflated her chest and inhaled the clean night air. To her the night air always tasted sweet. Inhaling it, she felt as if she were absorbing the beauty of the stars.

She reflected that there were many different types of people leading many different life styles in the world. She thought about destiny and fortune and came to the conclusion that no one could ignore or overlook the power of destiny which dominated their lives. She was not apprehensive about her destiny which was beyond human control. Even though disaster might be the result of destiny, she had special feelings for this inescapable phenomenon, given different sets of circumstances. She could feel a sort of wonder about nature. The art of survival was learned silently through the many hardships and bitter experiences in the course of one's life. She thought life itself was interesting, being systematically planned.

For instance, the owner of the general store had a problem with his son, Bong-chun. Bong-chun had given his father a hard time since he was little. He failed twice in elementary school and only completed his education with much difficulty. In fact, his father had to beg the school authorities for his son to receive his diploma. After leaving school Bong-chun spent his time in idleness, hanging around the theatre. He was a good dancer; he especially excelled in Russian folk dances, which required a good deal of tumbling and other delightful tricks. He was easy-going and cheerful; he got along well with all the world. Nothing upset or bothered him. However, he did not comply with his father's wishes. He chose to lead a hectic life style against his father's will. Whenever he got into trouble, his father tackled it in silence. He would frown deeply, and sometimes he was ready to cry but he managed to control himself by dusting or sweeping his store. The more his heart was troubled by his disappointing son the more meticulously he cleaned his store.

Young-sil knew all about Bong-chun and his strange relationship with his father. She saw their problem as an example of some stern law handed down from ancient times. She regarded their particular father-son relationship as quite normal and natural for them. How could it be otherwise for them? Young-sil had learned to rise above conditions which were far from ideal. She had also learned to look at all matters with a positive attitude. In other words, she took life as she found it and kept an open mind.

Young-sil could not exactly describe her state of mind about life and everything related to it. Yet she felt overwhelmed by her profound observations about it. She could not construct a theory about the way she felt. In this confused mood, she gazed at the star–studded, summer night sky. She had come to terms with world affairs, regardless of circumstance. She had gracefully accepted the basic facts of human life no matter how trivial they might seem, nor did she resent or complain about adversities.

She was now quite a distance away from the main road. Round the corner of the alley, she came upon Kyu-dong's house placed at the end of this alley. Her hut, like a big bird's nest, was perched on top of the stepping stones that rose vertically ten feet high off the ground. Odd-looking stones and small rocks of different shapes were piled on both sides of the stepping stones. It presented a bizarre sight like the Chonosek Pavilion. Children called it Diamond Mountain as a joke

Kyu-dong had been branded an 'unfit' woman among the village people. Since she had been abandoned by her husband, she had never spoken a word to anyone, and people now regarded her as a mute. Whenever people needed an extra hand, Kyu-dong was usually asked to work for them – on occasions such as weddings, birthdays, funerals or annual festivals. The only thing she could do well was polishing brassware. She worked very hard, not wasting even a minute; consequently, brassware polished by her was as shiny as silver.

Even when an employer told her she could stop polishing after doing an excellent job, Kyu-dong would pay no attention until she was satisfied. After the sun went down, then, she would quit her task and have a meagre supper behind the kitchen area. As soon as she finished her well-earned meal, she would leave the place immediately, leaving all the brassware on the ground; it had become her habit not to clean up the mess she had made before going home. The following day at the crack of dawn, Kyu-dong would return to her employer for her wages. She refused to accept silver nickels; she would take only copper coins. Her ignorance in insisting on getting small change made people sneer.

As Young-sil was passing Kyu-dong's hut, she could see a

55

dim light flickering. An infant's cry came from the hut. The road leading away from Kyu-dong's place was pitch black and Young-sil could see and admire the clear night sky. Suddenly, she thought of her friend, Soon-hee, and her father, Mr Choi, the fire station chief. The fire station was located right in front of the entrance to the marketplace. A tall watch tower, painted bright red, was built on top of the building, and two fire trucks were parked, almost facing the main road, ready to drive off at any minute. In a small, dimly lit room, adjoining the office, Soon-hee and her father shared living quarters. 'Soon-hee may be frightened when her father shows signs of insanity, yet when he returns to himself, I know she can depend on him.' Young-sil pondered on her friend's predicament. She felt sorry for her.

' Even though Soon-hee might live in fear of her father, she loved him and was good and faithful to him. She took care of him – cooking, washing, cleaning, working very hard to maintain a motherless household. Thinking of her friend's hard life, full of discomfort and hardship, Young-sil considered Soon-hee courageous and noble. She almost envied her dear friend's heroic determination to live with honour, yet at the same time she felt proud of her because she faced up to life's despairs and difficulties.

'Soon-hee's heart must be always immersed in sorrow,' Young-sil meditated. The feeling of envy she had for Soon-hee's devotion to her father possibly derived from her discovery that she herself did not belong to anyone yet. Her identity was, as far as she could see, vague and insignificant. Young-sil thought of her poor, ignorant parents and her older sister Sinn-sil as people by whom she could not be judged – as either good or bad. She felt acutely that they were too trivial to have any influence on her. There was no way they could control her or influence her destiny. Consequently, her life with her unimportant family was merely to be ignored. Though her life was far different from that of her friend Soon-hee, yet Young-sil was confident that she would be able to handle anything that required her attention or rise to any responsibility. She could handle matters just as well as Soon-hee, or perhaps even a lot better than Soon-hee. Young-sil felt ready to tackle any problem that needed solving; she could put it right with courage and dignity.

A delightful unexpected breeze blew up, tickling the hem of her skirt and putting her in such a good mood that she walked on, passing her own house in her mood of bliss. To her, her house represented just a place to sleep. Until she became drowsy, she did not feel it necessary to go home. Her parents' house was not a home where her heart was.

2

Young-sil had been told by her home-room teacher to stay behind after school. As soon as her last class was over, upset at this unpleasant order, she went to the teacher's room.

'Will you wait for me by the agricultural building?' Mr Chae asked in a low tone, shuffling papers on the desk, avoiding Young-sil's eyes. 'I'll be right over.'

'I know what you're up to, mister,' thought Young-sil. 'Before you know it, you'll be sacked by the school authorities. I just know it. People talk about you, don't you know?' Young-sil was not at all thrilled to be asked to wait for him; she thought it rather ridiculous, yet she obeyed him. She came out of the sandy hallway and walked toward the hill right behind the school.

She passed by the mulberry bushes. Years earlier, the school authorities had planted quite a few mulberry trees for the purpose of teaching the students how to raise silk worms. However, through the years this goal had never been realized. In fact, there had never been anyone to carry out the original plan of having a class to raise silk worms. The green leaves of the mulberry trees matured and withered gradually as the earth rotated on its axis. Beyond the mulberry fields were acacia woods. Acacia trees made one feel pleasant and light no matter how thick and luxuriant the trees were. Their rich appearance never ceased to give an impression of freshness. The acacia trees still were bearing milky-coloured flower petals here and there. The pathway under the twisted and tangled acacia branches resembled a tunnel. Slowly Young-sil turned in that direction. Suddenly, she felt stifled by the sweet fragrance of flowers and grass.

The tunnel-like road under the thick acacia branches was

tinted pale green by the magical play of sunlight. There were a few well-known rendezvous places for young lovers – the beach, a pine grove, or the secluded road through the acacia woods.

The school children loved to spread rumours about each other. They speculated about pretty girls and disreputable boys and the places they met. Their rumours might seem innocent, but sometimes they were quite malicious.

In this secluded place Young-sil recalled the face of the schoolboy, Kyung-sik Yoon. Her heart was filled with hazy happiness. She did not understand why she felt like this, half happy, half sad. Perhaps happiness was too much for her. Perhaps that was why she felt sad as well. She just could not fathom her own state of mind. She had already forgotten the embarrassing moment when she had come upon him on the seashore not long ago. All she remembered was how warmly he had looked at her. His kind and gentle gaze filled her mind. Yes, that boy Kyung-sik Yoon – he would always remain in her heart.

Young-sil was indignant that she had to wait for Mr Chae in a place like this. The more she thought about it, the more exasperated she became. Mr Chae was not one of her favourite people. From the first day she met him, she disliked him. His golden skin made him look sallow; he always appeared unhealthy. He gave the general impression of being unclean; however, his tone of voice was as smooth as if it were blended with wild honey.

'I don't understand at all how in the world my sister can find him attractive. What can she possibly see in him anyway?' Young-sil wondered desperately. She did not approve of Mr Chae as a man, and she doubted her sister's mentality in liking such a man. Yet, she realized that Sinn-sil could not afford to be too choosy when it came to selecting a man. Perhaps Sinn-sil was compliant with anyone who led her along, remaining absolutely passive herself.

After a short while, Mr Chae joined Young-sil. He gave her a broad grin. When he smiled, his mouth became a little slanted, forming a long line. She hated his sly smile. 'He makes me sick,' Young-sil thought. Mr Chae put his hand into the pocket of his sordid navy blue jacket and searched for something, making a rustling noise.

'Will you please deliver this letter to your sister? I'd really appreciate it.' Mr Chae handed her a white envelope. He was speaking in a phoney Seoul accent, which sounded awkward and ridiculous to her.

After handing her the letter, he closed his eyes dramatically as if he were acting in a play. Watching Mr Chae's ludicrous gestures, Young-sil thought of his family – his wife, his three-year-old son, and an infant who was always carried on its mother's back.

'What do you think of me, my dear Young-sil?' Mr Chae asked abruptly, starting to walk under the acacia trees. She lent a deaf ear to this unanswerable question.

Young-sil was not popular with her teacher because of her poor academic record. She was anything but a good student. She had no respect for Mr Chae, yet she realized he had some kind of power over his students, including herself.

'Oh, how unhappy I am,' Mr Chae exclaimed emotionally, 'and yet what a fortunate man I am!' Mr Chae's repeated exclamations gave Young-sil a creepy sensation. His red necktie, his untidy, long hair that covered part of his forehead, and his lips trembling as though he were overwhelmed by deep emotion – all these outward appearances disgusted Young-sil. Yet she could see dimly why her sister was attracted to this repulsive man. Perhaps her sister was drawn to Mr Chae's sly approach.

Young-sil experienced a sudden burning in her throat. It was certainly not a pleasant feeling; it was too intense. Anxious to escape, Young-sil made a low bow to Mr Chae and climbed the hill. 'I certainly am not going to deliver this letter to my sister. No way.' Young-sil crumpled up the letter and walked on rapidly.

On the way home she met Mr Soo-chul Chang, son of the wealthiest man in town. Young-sil was awed by his outward appearance; he looked like a different breed from Mr Chae or any of the ordinary men she saw every day. Even his black university uniform was impressive, glittering. He was studying at a university in Japan. His university cap was round, not like the square cap worn by Mr Chang the Sunday school teacher, the son of the restaurant owner. Mr Soo-chul Chang's round cap was far more stylish and becoming to him. The way he walked was different too – light and brisk. He was wearing beautiful shoes. Not only did he dress well, Mr Soo-chul Chang was very handsome. Young-sil was especially attracted by his large shining eyes. She could not keep her own eyes off him, feeling dazed and blinded by his glamorous appearance. Young-sil was taken aback to meet him unexpectedly in the middle of the street. Mr Soo-chul Chang passed her with a friendly smile. He seemed pleasant and happy. When he smiled she could see his well-set clean white teeth sparkling.

Young-sil was dizzy with a strange sensation – not sweet or tingling like her secret feeling for Kyung-sik Yoon. Yet it produced a startling effect on her heart. She was quite obsessed by her encounter with the handsome, rich, widely-envied Mr Chang, the town prince. When he passed Young-sil Mr Soo-chul Chang looked for a moment as if he were about to speak to her, but he walked briskly away.

Even after she reached home, and stood in front of her sister Sinn-sil, Young-sil could not conceal her bursting excitement.

'Hey, sister, guess who I saw on the way home from school? I'll give you one hint, though. You went out with him some time ago.'

Her sister merely looked at her for a second, and then resumed her sewing, bending her head low as if to ignore her sister's obstreperous approach. Sinn-sil's shining black hair was nicely braided again. The place where her father had cut her hair was well hidden by the remaining long tresses.

Young-sil threw down the crumpled envelope in front of her sister, even though she had promised herself not to deliver Mr Chae's letter. Perhaps meeting Mr Soo-chul Chang on the way home had changed her mind. To be exact, she was seized with an evil desire to hurt her sister's feelings. She felt like throwing a handful of dirt in her sister's face out of pure malice.

Sinn-sil glanced at the letter but she did not bother to pick it up. There was no response from Sinn-sil even though she knew who had sent it. She was as calm as she could be, completely ignoring the letter.

'Don't you want to read it?' Young-sil, asked loudly. 'Mr Chae asked me to give it to you.' Young-sil, irritated with her sister, did not even care whether her father might hear her or not.

Lowering her eyes, Sinn-sil entirely ignored her sister's deliberately unkind behaviour.

'Aren't you going to read it?' Young-sil urged her in a more gentle tone this time. She had just heard a sound coming from her father's room.

'Read it quickly. If you don't, my sister, I won't be able to go back to class tomorrow,' Young-sil explained. 'Mr Chae will punish me for not doing my errand for him.'

At her sister's entreaty, Sinn-sil got up slowly and picked up the letter. Then she went to her room, returning immediately. The letter must have been still unopened. Suddenly, Young-sil felt tired and frustrated at her sister's passive, aloof attitude and abruptly left her.

It was nearly a month after Young-sil brought Mr Chae's letter to her sister that Sinn-sil suddenly disappeared. No one knew where she was. No one knew when she had slipped out of the house. She did not return home even after dusk. Her father, Maan-kap Shin, raved with fury when he discovered Sinn-sil's absence. In a rage he ran in and out of the house and into the street.

'That ungrateful girl! Oh, what a wretched . . .' Mr Shin called her names in disgust and disappointment. His eyes were bloodshot; he recklessly threw anything he could lay his hands on, and kicked rice bowls and anything else he could find. Patiently Young-sil gathered up the scattered rice from the floor in the back room. Carefully she put the rice into a dried gourd and took it to the backyard. Slowly she ate the rice.

The following day there was still no sign of Sinn-sil. In vain Mr Shin waited for her return until darkness fell. When all hope of seeing her was gone, Mr Shin locked the door of his room and began to wail.

Before locking himself in his room in grief and disgust, Mr Shin had looked in the elementary school which was vacant for the summer vacation; and he had even gone to see Mr Chae, hoping for information about his daughter.

Mr Chae was in the middle of his courtyard when he was attacked by the furious father Mr Shin, who strangled him half to death. Convinced of Chae's innocence, however, Mr Shin became less desperate. Realizing he would get no information about his daughter from Mr Chae, he lost all inclination to inquire by force. After leaving Mr Chae's place, Mr Shin went to the beach and spent all night looking for his daughter.

As soon as she got up in the morning, Young-sil went to the front yard to await her mother's return. Her mother, carrying the water buckets, approached from the other side of the hill.

As soon as her mother walked into the courtyard, Young-sil blocked her way, demanding, 'Mother, please let me have one Won.'

'Are you out of your mind?' her mother shrieked. 'You'd better clear out of my way, child!' Surprisingly, her tone of voice was sharp and intense.

'I need that money; please give it to me, Mother. There's something I have to take care of with that money!' Young-sil insisted, repeating herself. Her mother rolled her eyes as if she were dumbfounded at her daughter's stubborn demand. As they were arguing, Mr Shin walked into the yard. Young-sil stepped back, discouraged by his unexpected appearance. Reluctantly, Young-sil left her mother.

'How can they be so foolish and senseless?' Young-sil wondered about her parents' mentality. She went to the kitchen and took a spoon. Without difficulty she opened the lock of a cedar chest with the head of the spoon. In the chest she found two one-Won notes carefully wrapped in cloth and placed between layers of clothes. Without hesitation, Young-sil took one of the notes and locked the padlock of the cedar chest again as if nothing had been taken.

With the one-Won note Young-sil went out into the street and walked towards the marketplace. At the country bus station, she bought a return ticket to a well-known hot spring spa.

3

The return ticket cost Young-sil 90 Chun. That left ten Chun for her; she spent five Chun on a packet of caramel at a Japanese sweet shop. First she took her time looking around the shop in which were displayed many wonderful, delightful goodies for children. The caramel packet was beautifully decorated in plum and gold colours, and was attractive enough to pass Young-sil's careful inspection. Young-sil wrapped the caramel box in her handkerchief and tied it carefully, as if it were a precious treasure.

The country bus with its huge tyres finally emerged from the garage on to the road. Young-sil was the very first to get on the bus; she found a seat in the centre. At first she thought of sitting on the front row but changed her mind, convinced that she would be better placed to observe people closely from the centre row.

At intervals people got on the bus, one by one. Young-sil recognized 'Bukchung Auntie' among the passengers. 'Bukchung Auntie' had got herself up presentably in a brand-new dress, and she was also carrying a long, flat handbag. Her new dress was not at all becoming, and her cream-coloured handbag, which was decorated with red beads around the snap, did not match her general appearance. If one of the barmaids in the restaurant carried such a small, delicate purse, it would look all right, thought Young-sil as she idly criticized her attire. Nevertheless, 'Bukchung Auntie' aroused Young-sil's immediate interest and curiosity, not just because she was the mother of the most handsome boy in town, but because she was also the heroine of the story told to Young-sil by Koo-bae's grandfather. Knowing how kind 'Bukchung Auntie' had been to Koo-bae's grandfather in his time of need made Young-sil feel close to this heavy-set woman almost as if she knew her personally. She wanted to ask her where she was going. Whether 'Bukchung Anutie' would respond or not, she was eager to speak to her, and she scrutinized her good-natured face closely. Young-sil hoped she might learn something about her son, Chang-kyu. However, she decided not to risk speaking to 'Bukchung Auntie', and looked outside in silence. She had made up her mind not to reveal the purpose of her trip to the hot spring in any circumstances, and thought it wiser to remain unnoticed in the bus.

As the bus conductress finally climbed aboard, the bus began to move its straining engine, its gears squeaking and creaking. The young conductress wore a navy blue sailor's cap with two ribbons hanging down her back, and carried a small leather money bag on her wide, sturdy belt. Young-sil looked at her for some time with apparent envy. Noticing Young-sil's admiring gaze, the girl arrogantly stuck her nose in the air and examined Young-sil from head to toe. Then, as if she were well-pleased with herself, she began to hum with a superior air:

'Come along, my dear friend,
Flowers are beckoning from the mountain ridge
Come along, my dear friend,. . .
Come and see,
Let us enjoy these beautiful wild flowers
Along the murmuring river . . . . . .'

The conductress hummed away as though proud of her talent. Young-sil could not help admiring her. She found it hard to hide her envy, imagining how pleasant it would be if she could show herself off like this girl, wearing a leather belt around her waist and singing happily as she leant against the bus door.

'Bukchung Auntie', sitting right in front of Young-sil, fell into conversation with an old woman across the aisle.

'Where are you going?' the woman asked.

'I'm going to Youngdong. How about you?'

'I'm going to have a steam bath. My head has been bothering me, you know. Tell me, is it true that you have purchased some land in Youngdong?'

'It's not a large plot,' 'Bukchung Auntie' replied gently.

'It really amazes me how in the world you can manage to buy so many acres in Youngdong.'

Suddenly, their conversation became more interesting. Young-sil, delighted at this change, paid close attention.

'How is your son? Is he doing all right?'

'Yes, he is just fine, thank you.'

'I saw him the other day. What a nice-looking young man he is. He gets more handsome every time I see him. You have a very fine son, I tell you.'

'Do you really think my son is good-looking?'

'Yes, I do. He's the best-looking boy in Wonjin.'

'To tell you the truth, everyone tells me that,' 'Bukchung Auntie' said with obvious pride and joy. She unwrapped a package and offered the woman some expensive sweets. Young-sil noticed the many different rings on her fingers – a gold band, a white gold ring, and a pearl ring. Even the bow of her blouse was smartly decorated with a lengthy gold chain.

As the women's conversation grew quieter, Young-sil pictured 'Bukchung Auntie's' son, Chang-kyu – his thick

64

eyebrows and flashing eagle eyes under his school cap which he always wore cocked to one side. His firmly closed mouth made him look tough. She thought of his dark complexion and smiled with an inner glow.

'You might have a hard time finding the right girl for your handsome son,' the old woman teased. Although she was an old woman, she sounded as if she understood the young man's mind.

'I know what you mean. I guess she will have to be a fine girl,' 'Bukchung Auntie' said with a laugh.

'She must be the fairest one of all.'

'I think my son has already got his eye on a girl. Last year he mentioned he likes Dr Baek's daughter. You know, the Seoul Clinic's doctor – his daughter. Anyway, she is very pretty and a good girl, too.'

'I know who you're talking about. Her name is Sung-aah, isn't it?'

'My son said he would like to marry her. His childish remark made me laugh, but I believe he was serious when he said that.'

'Oh, my word! Your son certainly has good taste in choosing a wife, I can tell you!' The women roared with hearty laughter.

Young-sil had become pale. She felt as though drained of her energy and strength when she overheard the name of her dear friend Sung-aah. Young-sil took no further interest in the two women's conversation. In her disappointment, she turned her head away.

The bus had already turned away from the beach and was through the mountains. Young-sil could see corn and potato fields here and there from the window. Plants were growing even along the rocky mountain slope.

The bus rambled along the rugged mountain road. It would take about two hours to reach 'C' hot spring, which was located at the end of the trail. This was the very first time that Young-sil had visited the spring, a well-known tourist attraction.

Even though Young-sil had chosen this particular place, she was still not one hundred per cent positive she would find her sister here. Her visit was a gamble, a last resort. She had no good reason for coming to this place.

Momentarily, fear and uncertainty assailed her heart. However, Young-sil managed to overcome them. Even though she might not locate her sister, she consoled herself with the hope that she might find something of value when she got there. Fear gave way to curiosity as the end of the journey approached. In truth, Young-sil's decision to visit this place was not entirely disinterested. She had always wanted to go to 'C' hot spring and now she had a legitimate reason to do so.

Her father, Maan-kap Shin, had been searching for his daughter literally from door to door, on the streets, over the mountains, on the seashore, and in amusement places. His search had been very time-consuming and all in vain. Young-sil felt it was safe to conclude that her sister must be staying somewhere away from Wonjin. She was certain that her school teacher, Mr Chae, had nothing to do with Sinn-sil's sudden disappearance. Young-sil, therefore, reasoned that her sister must have eloped with someone else. Had she run away to Seoul? But as Sinn-sil had taken nothing with her, Young-sil thought that her sister must still be somewhere near Wonjin. How could her sister, who had not taken even a change of clothes, stay away so long? She might have left home, intending to return the same day. Perhaps whatever she was doing was taking longer than she thought. Perhaps she could not get away from her business. Young-sil contemplated all these possibilities.

The wings of her fertile imagination spread at full span as she recalled her father's vain search which only confirmed Young-sil's theory that her sister must be out of town. And so she had decided to act upon this belief and try to find her herself.

The previous afternoon Young-sil had idly wandered near Mr Chang's house, recalling the day she had delivered Mr Chae's letter to her sister and had unexpectedly happened to run into Soo-chul Chang on the way home from school. She couldn't detect any sign of anyone near Mr Chang's house. In desperation, she wished Mr Chang's notorious dog would come out. If it did, the servant would run after the dog, risking his life. If that had happened, she would have spoken to the servant to find out if he knew anything.

However, neither the dog nor the servant came out. There was no trace of anyone. Young-sil was discouraged and was about to give up all hope. Just as she was about to leave,

Young-sil saw two of Mr Chang's daughters coming from the beach. They were half-sisters of Soo-chul Chang, daughters of his father's concubine. The girls were accompanied by a man. Young-sil was instantly elated at the sight of these girls, convinced she might learn something from them. The girls and the man were engaged in conversation which turned out to be very helpful to Young-sil.

'See you girls tomorrow.'

'Okay, tomorrow, then.'

'By the way, when did you say your brother would return?'

'I don't know for sure,' one girl laughed softly.

'What kind of friend is he?' the man complained mildly. 'Your brother asked me to join him here, and now look at him. He has gone off without me.'

'Well,' one girl responded, smiling, 'you should have known better. I mean you should have let my brother know before you came.'

The Chang girls, who attended a girls' high school in Seoul, were back home for the summer holidays. The man appeared to be from Seoul, too. Judging from their conversation, Young-sil concluded that the man was staying somewhere else even though he might have been invited to stay with Soo-chul Chang.

As soon as one girl went inside, the other sister and the man held hands eagerly and rubbed their shoulders together. After a few kisses, the other girl went inside, still giggling. The front gate clanged shut and was securely locked. Finally, the man, deeply flushed, glanced at Young-sil, who had been standing near him all this time. His eyes looked through her as if he were dreaming, and walked away with a strange expression on his face.

From their conversation she had learned that Soo-chul Chang was out of town, even though he had arranged for his friend to visit him. And that was why she was going in search of her sister at 'C' hot spring even though she could not be certain that her theory was absolutely correct.

Young-sil was recalled to the present in the bus. Quite a few people had already got off, including 'Bukchung Auntie' and the old woman. Young-sil and two others were the only passengers left in the bus as it rumbled on up the valley, where the scenery was breathtaking. Young-sil's heart swelled with contentment and admiration as she gazed in rapture at the magnificent mountain vista and the winding country road which looked as neat and clean as if they had been washed by a rolling stream. She admired the sight of the numerous river beds with their white round stones and pebbles. She could feel the stillness and cleanness of the valleys, rivers and mountains.

The mood of the valley was gentle and natural, unlike the unpredictable temperament of the sea. In contrast to the solitude and serenity of the mountains, the valley offered warmth and closeness. It was a totally different world, which she would never have seen if she had not come to search for her sister. Just for a moment, however, she pictured her indignant father. He might harshly scold and punish her, pulling her hair in anger. Yet this did not bother her very much; she was not afraid of her father or of possible punishment.

'Ladies and gentlemen, we are finally at our destination,' the conductress announced. 'Please get off at this point and be careful. Thank you.'

Before anybody else could get off, the girl jumped off the bus. Around the bus station a few houses were scattered here and there; however, Young-sil could see other houses some distance away.

The sun dazzled her eyes as she walked along the road in the strong heat of high noon. She could feel the dry heat radiating from the soil. Dark pinkish hollyhocks in full bloom along the road made a pleasant sight for passers by.

Young-sil made her way into the village, not knowing exactly what to do when she got there. She had no idea where to begin looking for her sister and Mr Soo-chul Chang. She decided to try the hotels and inns in the village first.

As she walked down to the village, she found a small mossy fountain under a big tree. She sat down on the grass by the inviting fountain and began to sample the caramel she bought at the Japanese store. Deliberately she took time to appreciate the delicious new taste. It simply melted in her mouth. Young-sil thought she would never complain about the world as long as it provided her with constant surprises and wonderful things like the caramel. Satisfied, she got up and started to walk down to the village in a relaxed manner. Since Soo-chul Chang was one of the wealthiest men in town, she reasoned, he and her sister must be in a first-class hotel.

She soon spotted a high-class Japanese hotel in the centre of the village. She entered through the side door of the hotel; no one seeemed to notice her. Relieved, Young-sil took off her shoes and walked down the hallway past the main hall and several guest rooms and a spacious kitchen. As she walked along the hall, she could see a side hallway leading to public bathing rooms. The pool-size bathtub surprised her; she saw that a small private bath was also available.

Young-sil peeped in each bathroom through the window; she even dared to open the glass door to look for her sister. Most of the baths were empty. One or two were being used by Japanese women. Seeing their clothing scattered about in the clothes baskets, she did not bother to look further. After walking up and down the hall a few more minutes, she gave up her search in that hotel. Fortunately, she easily found her way back to the entrance to the first hall where she had left her shoes.

In the same manner Young-sil searched several more hotels and Korean inns to find her sister. At Korean inns, Young-sil made enquiries from the owner, about her sister. However, all her efforts turned out in vain. She could not find her sister anywhere in this strange village.

Even in the sultry summer heat, there were quite a few patrons of the hot springs to be seen; they strolled along the clean, spacious, well-kept banks along the shallow brook. Some were equipped with fishing rods, ready to try their luck. Young-sil concluded that her sister had not come here in the first place; even if she were here, Young-sil thought, it would be very difficult to find her in such crowds.

After being harshly scolded by a Japanese manager for snooping about his hotel, Young-sil gave up altogether. To refresh herself, she went to the shallow brook and bathed. She made up her mind to make the best of this journey. With her last 5 Chun Young-sil bought a bean-jam bun, hoping to relieve her empty stomach. One single bun did not satisfy her hunger, but it made her feel a lot better. She was even content to recollect the whole day's adventure in this strange place.

When now dusk began to gather, Young-sil left the village

to catch the bus. She passed an empty plot on the way to the country bus station. The cultivated land was choked with weeds, and clover was flowering in abundance. As Young-sil walked along, the back of a wooden building came into sight. It must have been the rear of a public bath house. Hot steam was coming out of a small high window.

Irresistably her feet led her to the wooden building which was painted light blue. In order to peep through the window, she piled up scattered cans, stones, and boxes to stand on. The window was still too high for her to reach. She rearranged the crumpled boxes and piled them vertically. She managed to find a spot where she could put her feet on a wooden fence. Finally, she hung on the wall and peeped through the steamy window.

The shock she received made her lose her balance and she fell on the grass. She sat up vacantly, feeling stunned. The scene she had just witnesed was so traumatic that she could not recover her senses. She could hardly think at all. After a while, she got up, remembering that there was one more thing she had to find out – who was that light-skinned woman she had just seen? Was it her sister Sinn-sil? Who was the man holding the woman in his arms? Was it Soo-chul Chang? Young-sil only knew one thing for certain – she had to find out who these mysterious people were.

She rubbed her hands with saliva and climbed the wooden boxes again, with caution. The boxes under her feet started to sway uncontrollably. She balanced herself, shifting her weight from side to side. When she finally managed to reach the window pane again, the posture of the man and woman had completely changed.

Sinn-sil was sitting on the smooth edge of the round, tiled bath tub. Her sister's profile was half hidden by her long hair, hanging down her shoulder. Her eyes seemed to be dreaming – gazing into the distance. The bathhouse was dimly tinted a rosy colour by the direct rays of twilight. Even Sinn-sil's naked body was coloured in a mysteriously indescribable shade of pink.

Sinn-sil was bending down, almost covering her breast with one arm. Her posture reminded Young-sil of the statue of a Greek goddess that she had seen in the hall of her friend Sung-aah's house. From her shoulders to her ankles, the lines of

Sinn-sil's beautiful body were perfectly exquisite. Young-sil was almost dazzled by her sister's fiawless beauty. Her smooth, soft, vibrant skin matched the grace of her blossoming youth. Such absolute beauty frightened Young-sil – this could not be her own sister or a fellow human being. There was something almost holy in her sister's statuesque beauty.

Such breathtaking beauty, Young-sil felt, should be venerated, not violated by anyone. Young-sil sighed deeply from the bottom of her heart. She glimpsed the face of Soo-chul Chang. It did not really matter any more to her who the man was. It was enough that he was the man who had won her sister.

She climbed down and sat on the grass for a little while. A clear stillness eveloped her as she tried to recover from what she had seen. The pleasant, strong odour of the grass rose into the crimson evening sky. Without warning, Young-sil was engulfed with happiness. All the way home the mood lasted. Every once in a while, she would shake her head and she smiled continually.

The next morning Young-sil tried to relieve her father's anxiety.

'You don't need to worry about Sinn-sil, Father. I am sure she is with Soo-chul Chang, and is in good hands.'

Young-sil stepped back, looking at her father with fear. She expected a blow from his angry fist at any moment. She expected him to take out his frustration and anger on her by exclaiming: 'What are you talking about? You and your sister are the daughters of a whore.'

Amazingly, however, her father looked at Young-sil blankly as if he had lost his senses.

'Is she all right? Is she still alive?' her father mumbled. That was the only response her father made. His eyes became bloodshot, and he quickly left his younger daughter.

All day long her father remained in his room, not bothering Young-sil with further questions. 'How strange!' Young-sil wondered about her father's unpredictable behaviour. She simply could not understand him.

Unlike her father, however, her mother, usually so quiet and controlled, exhausted her daughter with many detailed questions.

Summer in the northern harbour city is shorter than in other places. As summer was about to bid farewell, Sung-aah's household was filled with an approaching festival mood. Her grandmother was going to celebrate her sixtieth birthday. The preparation of her birthday banquet had been in progress now for several days. Whenever there was any kind of celebration, it was the custom in Wonjin to summon Kyu-dong to polish the brass. Thus, the beginning of the festival was marked by Kyu-dong's arrival. Before the sun dispersed the thick wall of dawn, Kyu-dong left her small hut. Strange-looking stones and rocks lined both sides of the narrow stone steps below her hut.

Kyu-dong descended the stone steps and walked briskly toward Sung-aah's house to fulfil her task. Since she realized her own limitations, she had never tried to expand or heighten her mental capacity by seeking knowledge to better herself. Nevertheless, she had an excellent sense of direction. She knew exactly where she was supposed to go and found her destination without any difficulty. She had a bronze-coloured, muddy-looking complexion. Her hair was always pulled into a round knot and secured by a grubby red ribbon. Her blouse was short and tight, showing her well-developed breasts.

'How is your child? Is he doing all right?' the other women asked Kyu-dong. as she sat polishing the brassware, panting heavily on a straw mat in the front courtyard. She turned a deaf ear.

'Good God!' a woman exclaimed emotionally. 'Why didn't He give a child to detective Kim and his mistress, who want a child so desperately? Why did He give a son to a retarded woman like Kyu-dong? I simply don't understand His doings!'

'I agree with you,' another woman replied. 'And what about the second wife of a rich old man who's dying?' The rest of the women stopped working and laughed softly at this new topic of converstation.

'Whatever happened to that household anyway? Is the old man still hopelessly sick?'

'I'm afraid so. Every day his second wife goes to see him in his room. She cries her eyes out. As soon as she comes out of the room, his first wife's son goes to see him. Both of them take turns trying to overhear what the other one's saying in the old man's room. What a way to live!'

'I understand the old man can't say a word anyway, so what's the use of bothering him?'

'I'm sure he's as alert as anyone. His great fortune depends solely on his signature. A signed letter will determine his inheritance. It is crucial, you know, for the old man to act in some way soon.'

'If that's true, I bet no one can sleep at night in peace. You can't when your mind is occupied by something else, you know.'

'Sleep? Are you kidding?' One woman laughed cynically. 'His second wife looks ready to die with worry.'

These women never stopped talking as they worked in the kitchen but they never stopped working either. Sung-aah's grandmother, a widow, smiled at them in her gentle way.

'You're a great help in this hot weather: we really appreciate it,' she said sincerely. 'Thank you very much.' She had special compassion for Kyu-dong. She had willingly given her her old clothes and rewarded her with plenty of sweets and biscuits. However, at the end of the day, Kyu-dong took only the sweets and biscuits home. The clothes Sung-aah's soft-hearted grandmother gave her were left on the mat untouched.

Before she gave birth to her son, Kyu-dong used to consume all the sweets on the way home. In fact, she was so obsessed with the delicious taste that she used to walk clumsily, hunching her shoulders in the gathering dusk. However, now that she had a son, Kyu-dong saved everything for him. She did not allow herself to eat even one piece of candy.

Women clucked their tongues approvingly, saying, 'What a good mother she is to think of her child like that . . .'

Finally, the day of Sung-aah's grandmother's sixtieth birthday banquet arrived. Her house teemed with guests and well-wishers, dressed in their best. It seemed as if the whole town was present. The élite of the town – school principal, community committee members – were among the guests. Detective Kyung-boo Kim and fire chief Mr Choi mingled with the priest, church elders and Koo-bae's grandfather. The owner of the barber shop, 'Bukchung Auntie', and even a well-known VD patient were also among the big crowd. It appeared that the only ones who didn't show up were Kyung-sik, his mother and the notorious high-class prostitute Ae-kyung.

The celebration party went on all day long – morning, afternoon and evening. People came and went as they pleased and were provided with plenty of food, fun and gaiety. Fresh fruits were rare in Wonjin; yet Sung-aah's thoughtful mother had managed to acquire plenty for the guests. She was able to offer them ice-cold watermelons, peaches and melons. Endless fruits were brought on a large tray to please everyone, and plenty of rice cakes as well. The Sunday school teacher, Mr Chang in his gold-rimmed glasses, was working hard to seat everyone in their proper place. His manner of guiding people was reminiscent of his way of conducting his church choir on Sundays. Mr Chang held his handkerchief in his right hand, perspiring heavily. He never ceased to smile and cheerfully greeted everyone no matter how busy he became.

'Will you come this way, please? I trust you and your family are well. Please come this way,' Mr Chang greeted each guest in his pleasant manner as he showed them to their seats.

Young-sil had not been formally invited, but she made a point of coming to the banquet anyway. She could not even imagine not being a part of such a joyous occasion, especially since she was such a good friend of Sung-aah. All day long Young-sil tagged along with Sung-aah and made twice as much fuss of her friend.

As night fell, children who had come with their parents mixed with the uninvited village children and they mingled with the well-wishers; all became one at heart and helped to celebrate this happy occasion in their own way. They made their own party in the corner of the front courtyard, illuminated by the full moon. As Bong-chun, the son of the general store owner, began a Russian dance, the children began to clap and sing in delight.

Young-sil had been watching 'Bukchung Auntie's' son, Chang-kyu, for quite some time now. He leaned against the wall, his shining eyes fixed on one spot. As one boy clumsily played his harmonica, Chang-kyu took it away from him and played it well. Young-sil watched him with admiration as if she were carried away by his music. He played 'Santa Lucia' so splendidly that he immediately captured her heart. The exotic melody was light, yet stimulating; she was touched by its

74

romantic sensation. Her heart pounded as she watched Chang-kyu leaning against the wall and playing the harmonica, moving his shoulders slightly to the tune.

Young-sil was bewildered by the realization that she was helplessly attracted to Chang-kyu. Even though he had a bad reputation, she was willing to overlook his shortcomings: his expulsion from school for not obeying school rules; he had been caught attending the theatre. He now attended the Boys' Middle School in a neighbouring town. She did not care what other people thought of him. All that mattered to her was that Chang-kyu was a handsome boy who stirred her heart. Chang-kyu returned the harmonica to the owner and slipped away unnoticed. When she realized he was no longer there, Young-sil left the party and tried to find him, looking everywhere. Finally, she came upon Chang-kyu facing Sung-aah in the shade near the store room. Neither of them saw her and she stepped back into the shadows.

'Take this please,' Chang-kyu offered Sung-aah a small, rectangular parcel.

'Is it a present for my grandmother?' Sung-aah asked, accepting the gift with some reluctance.

'No, it's for you, just for you.'

Sung-aah looked at him in dismay. She appeared nonplussed by this unexpected gift from Chang-kyu and tried to give it back to him. 'No, really . . . please take this back.'

'All right, then,' he conceded, smiling gently. 'Why don't you give it to your grandmother if that would make you feel better?' Chang-kyu departed quickly before Sung-aah could say anything else. She stood dazed, biting her left fist. Her head was silhouetted on the lighter part of the ground. Young-sil decided to make her presence known.

'Hello, there, Sung-aah, what have you got in your hand?' she called.

'This? Oh, it's nothing,' Sung-aah seemed embarrassed.

'Let me see, then,' Young-sil insisted, reaching out her hand to touch it. Sung-aah hesitated and, appeared confused. Ignoring her friend's feelings, Young-sil took the box from Sung-aah.

'Come on, Sung-aah, let's look at this together,' Young-sil started walking towards the store house that was clearly visible under the full moon.

As soon as she reached it Young-sil sat down with the box in her lap and began to unwrap it eagerly. She never could restrain her curiousity, and now she could not wait to see what she would find when she unwrapped the package. A pale blue box met her eager eyes. Somehow she felt sure that some kind of expensive, precious toy would emerge from the box. The possibility excited her immensely. Her heart beat rapidly with anticipation. In comparison, her friend merely stood with her hands behind her back and watched Young-sil impassively.

'Look, look at this! Look how carefully it's been wrapped several times with soft tissue!' At last, after lengthy unwrapping, the contents was revealed: it was a small lamp with a pearl-coloured shade trimmed with shiny gold. The oil container was finished with pale jade green enamel. Even though it was only an ornament, Young-sil was enchanted with its delicate design and fine craftsmanship. She thought she had never seen anything so beautiful.

'Oh, my word!' Young-sil whispered in awe. She sighed softly, very impressed. The mysterious pearly colour of the lamp shade made Young-sil think of a distant fantasy land full of rich and extravagant things. In this dreamy mood, Young-sil held the delicate ornament tightly as if she didn't want to part with it.

'This surely is a treasure, a precious treasure,' Young-sil exclaimed excitedly while her friend gazed at the lamp with indifferent eyes. As she noticed Sung-aah's gentle gaze, Young-sil suddenly became possessed by ill temper.

'Who in the world gave you this, Sung-aah?' Young-sil asked rudely raising her eyebrows. She could not understand why she felt so cross with her friend. Sung-aah remained silent, merely looking up at the full moon. She appeared to be lost in thought. Her attitude reminded Young-sil of someone else. She persisted: 'Did someone give this to you?' Again, Sung-aah paid no attention.

'What will your mother say if you bring this strange gift home? Do you think she'll be cross with you?'

Sung-aah made no response, remaining still and silent.

'Surely your mum will ask who gave it to you, won't she?' Sung-aah remained mute.

'I wish I had something as fine as this for my own,' Young-sil hinted cunningly. Sung-aah seemed to be lost in another world, saying nothing, acknowledging nothing. Her lack of response, finally got through to Young-sil. Abruptly she fell silent herself and began to rewrap the lamp back in its crumpled paper. A deep sigh escaped her. Unexpectedly, Sung-aah's hand gently took the lamp from Young-sil's hand and held it up with as much care as she would a valuable treasure while she examined it with keen interest.

'Young-sil, my dear friend,' Sung-aah said at last, 'if you want this, you're welcome to have it. It's yours.' Her tone of voice was soft and low. Sung-aah's graciousness made Young-sil feel small and cheap. For a moment she overcame her childish greed; and shame transcended her wild desire to possess the delicate toy. Willingly and with pleasure Sung-aah handed the lamp to her friend, not because she was intimidated by Young-sil's aggressiveness nor because of her love for her friend, but for reasons of her own.

Young-sil realized that Sung-aah had wisely decided not to accept Chang-kyu's gift. She realized that she had no right to keep something that was given not to her but to Sung-aah. Yet the joy of acquiring something so beautiful eclipsed her scruples and already she had forgotten the shame she had momentarily felt when her friend showed her unselfishness. In fact, she was bursting with excitment. The only thing she cared about was the toy lamp in her hand. In ecstasy, she clasped it close to her breast.

'Thanks, I'll always treasure it,' Young-sil whispered.

A silent smile spread over Sung-aah's composed face as if she were pleased to make her friend happy by offering her the toy lamp. Yet, Young-sil could sense that her friend was really thinking of something else. She seemed to be in a world of her own, smiling a mysterious smile.

*   *   *

Sung-aah's grandmother's celebration party continued well into the next day overflowing on to the beach. The intention was to allow people to enjoy themselves in the cool air near the ocean. Children would swim and older people would cool off by getting just their feet wet.

A huge tent was erected and smooth straw mats were brought along with plenty of food. The guests were mostly close friends of Sung-aah's grandmother. The town's élite and the younger generation who were invited had politely declined. Consequently, the majority of people at the party on the beach were relatives and close friends. Somehow, Young-sil predicted she would see Chang-kyu at this close-knit party.

With the blazing sunlight beaming down on top of her head, Young-sil found her feet eagerly carrying her towards the sun-swept beach. The blinding sun exerted its power, in the middle of the day. Young-sil loved the sensation of treading upon the blistering hot sand under her bare feet.

The blue sea was usually angry and restless. Waves capped with white foam roared like angry lions, soaring high as the tall mountain in the air and hiding people playing in the ocean.

Young-sil immediately spotted Chang-kyu and Sung-aah near the tent. Sung-aah was smartly dressed in a pale blue dress. Her wide-brimmed white hat was well starched and very becoming. In fact Sung-aah looked absolutely ravishing in her outfit. Taking no notice of Chang-kyu, Sung-aah seemed to be very busy taking care of her grandmother. Chang-kyu was lying on the sand, staring at Sung-aah intensely. As the old women joyfully began to sing hymns in unison, Chang-kyu got up swiftly and walked into the shallow sea. He faced a huge wave that began to arc and then crashed down in a thunderous roar. The surf blocked him from view; whenever the waves subsided, his head could barely be seen. He disappeared under the water, his head bobbing further and further away.

'Oh, my goodness,' one woman exclaimed. 'Look at that boy! He's in danger!' At her excited remark, a few people turned to look at him. Chang-kyu was now hardly visible in the distance.

'Who can it be?' one woman asked in a concerned tone. 'Does anyone know who that is in the ocean?' Finally, the women stopped singing their hymn and paid a little more attention to the disappearing Chang-kyu.

'Isn't it the son of Bukchung Auntie?' one woman replied. 'I saw him lying on the sand not long ago.'

'Yes, of course; you're right. That's him. If his mother knew what he was doing, I am sure she would faint.'

'Goodness, gracious! I can't see him any more, not even a speck. Where is he, anyway?'

78

'Did you say someone's in the sea?' a third woman joined in. 'I can't see anyone out there.'

Finally, Sung-aah's grandmother took notice of the women's vocal apprehension. As soon as she realized what was going on, she turned pale, struck with fear, and dashed to the shoreline in anguish to sound the alarm and ask people to look for the missing boy. The Sunday school teacher, Mr Chang, gathered together several men and formed a search party. They rushed to the edge of the water and looked out to sea, but Chang-kyu was nowhere to be seen. Sung-aah's grandmother sent someone for her son, Dr Baek. People began to panic and talk about an evil omen. They apparently feared the worst.

Whenever the waves swept the sea sand, seemingly carefree urchins could be seen here and there in the shallow water, riding the dancing waves gleefully. There was no sign of Chang-kyu anywhere on the horizon. As the watchers on the shore reached a climax of fear and anxiety, a tiny black spot appeared in the distant ocean. It was Chang-kyu. Nearer, and nearer he swam, occasionally hidden by the towering waves. As they began to see him clearly, everyone heaved a deep sigh of relief.

'It's by God's grace that he returns to us safe and sound!' someone exclaimed.

'You're absolutely right,' the others agreed.

Now the party could resume its mood of celebration again after all the commotion. People busied themselves preparing the lunch table that had been temporarily forgotten; they ate, drank, and laughed in merriment.

Chang-kyu, looking angry and ill-tempered, walked straight ashore, not looking at anyone or anything, still panting heavily. As soon as he reached the sandy beach, he nearly collapsed. He rested there for a while and then began to put on his clothes, not bothering to brush the sand off from his sticky body, as if he were ready to go home. In silence, he walked past Sung-aah and turned his head round to look at her after he had passed. Then he turned and approached Sung-aah, again without hesitation. He seemed very sure of himself, yet he looked sad as he unfolded his fist, revealing a tiny cherry-coloured shell covered with sand in his hand. However, as he realized that Sung-aah was showing no interest and

79

not responding to him, Chang-kyu left her in silence, appearing very downcast.

Young-sil thought of the ornamental lamp that Sung-aah had given her the previous night. Young-sil kept her little treasure safe somewhere in her room. Strangely, however, she did not treasure it any more; somehow, its value to her had vanished.

The waves continued to roar, deafening the ears; the blazing sun baked the earth as if it wanted to set everything ablaze.

Chapter Three
AUTUMN

1

'Hisaya, what are you staring at?' asked Chun-mo, the barber's son.

Chun-mo had a clear, carefree voice which was reminiscent of the sound made by a strong wind passing by a hollow tree. Hisaya turned his head to acknowledge Chun-mo with narrowed eyes. He then flattened the surface of the dried grass with his fist and resumed his original posture, lying on his stomach and supporting his chin with his two hands. Hisaya had been lying on his stomach on the grass near the precipice on Chunma Mountain for quite some time, staring at the horizon. His white sweater was bright in the sunlight; he seemed to be in a state of hazy happiness like a contented, drowsy cat in the sunshine. Chun-mo lowered himself down on the grass by his friend and buried his chin in his cupped hands, copying little Hisaya.

Chun-mo's question demanded no answer; it was merely a signal that he was there and wanted recognition. Chun-mo was husky and strong. He was now lying on his stomach like his little friend, thrusting his broad, well-developed torso towards the edge of the cliff.

The sea, whipped to fury by the restless, roaring waves, was hundreds of feet below the cliff. The raging sea was like a frightening beast, inflicting deadly wounds while struggling instinctively for survival. The sight was unnerving and horrible. The rushing waves with their irresistible force battered the rough, mossy rocks and then returned to the sea with renewed fury and savagery. The restless waves produced an incredibly loud noise and the wind carried their threatening cries into the air. The deafening noise seemed to intimidate even the sun, driving away its bright smile and dimming its shine whenever the fuming, fitful waves splashed its face. The thick, white, foamy currents of water swept swiftly around the dark rocks, an awesome sight that gave spectators goose pimples and made them step back involuntarily at the first glance.

Nevertheless, Hisaya loved to visit this place; it did not frighten him at all. Even Chun-mo did not seem to be affected by the threatening sea below. They often came here to gaze at the horizon; in fact, they could spend all day there dreaming. They did not share their feelings with each other. They were satisfied just looking at the sea, lying on their stomachs. They were especially fascinated with the fluffy white clouds like candy-floss which clung on the horizon.

After a while Chun-mo turned round, twisting his torso slightly to face Hisaya.

'I went to church yesterday, Hisaya,' he announced proudly. Half of his entire body was erect, and, as he turned he lifted his legs high in the air. He did not seem to mind maintaining such a precarious posture.

'Did you?' Hisaya replied indifferently. Since he began living in the parsonage, nothing relating to church could impress him. It was simply not interesting enough to hold his attention.

However, Hisaya had plenty of interest and affection for his friend. So he looked encouragingly at Chun-mo, who seemed to be deep in thought.

'Do you know I went to the mountain all by myself the day before yesterday, Hisaya?' Chun-mo began grinning happily. As he smiled broadly, his thin, yellowish moustache cast a curious shadow on his face.

'Did you?' Hisaya said again, getting up slowly. Hisaya and Chun-mo sat on the edge of the cliff, turning their backs to the ocean. Suddenly, a crisp, cool autumn wind from the valley engulfed them. This chilly wind was quite unlike the warm, sticky wind from the sea they knew so well. As the wind blew, the tall, harshly dried and discoloured weeds quivered violently.

'You know what, Hisaya?' Chun-mo spoke again. 'I saw a bunch of azaleas in full bloom on the mountain.'

'Azaleas bloom in the springtime,' Hisaya smiled, making deep dimples. 'What you saw were maple trees, not azaleas.'

'I see,' Chun-mo lowered his head again, indicating his preoccupation with another idea. Unlike his well-developed body, his mentality was very limited. The most frightening experience he had ever had was being dragged by his parents to the state-run hospital, and going to Chinese doctors for acupuncture and heat treatment. As a result he detested any kind of medical treatment. It scared him so much that he would not speak to any adult, believing any adult would hurt him physically. Consequently, he made friends only with small, innocent children. Sometimes, naughty urchins made fun of him. Whenever Chun-mo encountered such children, he would usually disappear quietly. Yet he never bore a grudge aginst these unkind youngsters.

'I saw my girl, Jung-sun, in a pretty dress, standing in the middle of the azaleas,' Chun-mo said. 'She lowered her head and bowed like this to me.' Chun-mo smiled brightly. He beamed and became aglow whenever he spoke of his dream girl, Jung-sun.

Hisaya knew all about Chun-mo's dream girl, for he loved to talk about her all the time. In his fantasy, Jung-sun was always dressed beautifully and always gave him a splendid smile. Even though the setting frequently changed, his dream girl remained the same, always smiling invitingly. When Chun-mo talked about his girl, he soon found himself at the end of his inventive powers. He did not know what to say next. Hisaya knew all this by heart anyway.

'Tell me more about Jung-sun,' he said.

'She is a beautiful girl, my girl.'

'What does she look like?'

'Beautiful of course.'

'What kind of dress does she wear?'

'A spotless white dress.'

Chun-mo narrowed his eyes, apparently dreaming. The tiny wrinkles round his eyes conveyed the sense of his limited yet untroubled life style.

'Where does she live? Does she live near you?' Chun-mo shook his head emphatically. He always responded in this way when Hisaya questioned him about his fantasy girl. Hisaya was accustomed to Chun-mo's unvarying response; therefore, Hisaya soon lost interest in Jung-sun. He had given up hope of finding out who this mysterious girl was a long time ago. But, to please his friend, Hisaya decided to ask him one more question.

'Did you give Jung-sun your handkerchief?'

'No,' Chun-mo replied. All of a sudden, he looked serious, staring at Hisaya thoughtfully. 'I left it at home by mistake,' he mumbled, taking out a carefully folded handkerchief from the inside pocket of his jacket. The lacy handkerchief had a beautiful flower pattern. Chun-mo unfolded the handkerchief and looked at it carefully, then he pressed it against his heart.

'From now on, don't leave your handkerchief at home, in case, you meet Jung-sun,' Hisaya counselled his friend. Chun-mo nodded his head seriously. They now sat facing the sea, dangling their feet over the cliff edge.

'Look over there,' said Hisaya, pointing. 'Do you see that small boat sailing on the surface? I bet it's really a big ship.'

Chun-mo looked sideways at Hisaya and grinned with pleasure. Hisaya could not imagine what had made his friend suddenly so happy.

'My mother said there are countless streetcars, trains, and cars in Japan,' Hisaya exclaimed proudly. 'Big red and yellow streetcars. What do you think of that?'

'Did you say red and yellow streetcars?' Chun-mo asked, greatly impressed. He gazed excitedly at the distant horizon, kissed by soft, silvery clouds.

'Do you think if we go beyond the horizon, we'll see the red and yellow streetcars?' Chun-mo inquired, pointing to the horizon. Infected by his friend's enthusiasm and excitement, Hisaya was tempted to show him the red and yellow streetcars that he was told about.

Chun-mo was easy-going and so simple that it was easy to please him. Nothing was too small to gratify him. Even a very small kindness touched his heart deeply. He never passed

Hisaya without speaking to him whenever he met him in the street. Chun-mo cherished Hisaya's friendship.

'Do you think we can go over there?'

'Of course, we can go, on a big ship.'

'Oh, I'd love to go there.'

'Me, too. But if we go, don't you think your parents will come looking for you?'

At Hisaya's realistic question, Chun-mo swiftly jumped up in fear. His mind was suddenly clouded by the memory of his experience in the state hospital. The menacing face of a long-bearded doctor came into his mind as Hisaya mentioned his parents.

'I'm going to go and see the red and yellow streetcars. I want to see them for myself,' Chun-mo stated with determination.

'Wait,' Hisaya got up, too. 'Wait for me. I'll come with you.'

Dried leaves clinging to his trousers were blown away by the chilly breeze. From that day, Hisaya and Chun-mo never returned to the cliff on Chunma Mountain. As a matter of fact, they were never seen anywhere again.

*   *   *

Chun-mo's parents were hysterical upon learning of their son's disappearance. Church people came to console the grief-stricken parents. They also prayed for Chun-mo and his parents in special services.

The pastor prayed for Hisaya and his wife wept for her little, lost soul. Strangely, his own mother was unmoved by the loss of her son. To her, men were the be-all and end-all of her life. The only thing that mattered to her was to enjoy life as much as possible, no matter to her what it cost her or what others had to pay for her life style.

As long as she was sexually satisfied, she seemed quite content. For her lovers she prepared wine and hung an alluring red light in her room. She showered herself with perfume and closed the thick curtains, consumed with passion. Only when passion was satisfied was she at peace with the world. Her consuming passion belied her elegant, cool, outward appearance which was like that of a white lily in the field. She was a born coquette, drawing men to her like a

85

magnet. Whenever she flirted with one, she would lean against the man's chest, closing her eyes halfway. It used to drive them crazy with desire. Kyung-sik's father, for instance, the law school graduate, once a devoted husband and Christian, had wasted his life in his passion for her. Loving her in this blind, crazy way, he had destroyed himself and his family. Ae-kyung cared nothing about that. Children were a nuisance, anyway.

To her, the disappearance of Hisaya was as meaningless and insignificant as the passing wind against the windowpanes.

2

The moon shone brightly in the cold, clear autumn night, its stillness broken only by the cricket's song and the sound of fulling.

Kyung-sik held a skein of thread between his fingers and slightly moved his torso as his mother wound cotton thread on a spool. His mother's eyes were red as if she had been crying. Her straight pointed nose seemed to suggest her habitual state of sorrow. Under the dim light, her nose stood out prominently, casting a shadow on her pale cheek.

'Son, that's enough for tonight,' she said, gathering up her sewing materials. 'You can go to bed now.'

Kyung-sik made no reply to his mother's kind suggestion. Whenever his mother made the effort to speak, he felt that she was trying extremely hard to control her unhappiness and anxiety. She spoke with painful difficulty as if she had to fight to make the words come out. Because of this pain he sensed in his mother, Kyung-sik wished she would never talk. He could not endure to see her suffer. Generally speaking, his mother preferred to remain silent; she seldom said much except to inquire about his health. Apart from him she had lost her interest in life. She lived alone and faced her problems alone.

Kyung-sik was tempted to say, 'It's getting late, Mum. Why don't you go to bed, too?' but he restrained himself, fearing he might upset her even more. He wished he could do something to ease her burden of loneliness and unhappiness.

All he could do was to pull out several needles from the pin cushion and thread them for her. Even though she was only in her early thirties, her eyesight was poor, and her heavy sewing load each day made it worse. She had a difficult time threading needles at night; however, she refused to wear glasses. Several times Kyung-sik glanced furtively at the expression on his mother's face. He was suddenly gripped with the desire to tell her his plan, which he had been seriously contemplating for some days. Yet in spite of his longing to speak, his voice remained in the back of his throat, refusing to come out.

Although she could feel his intense gaze, his mother took no notice, as if she wished to be left alone. Perhaps she was afraid of what he might say.

'Mother,' Kyung-sik finally found his voice. 'I have a plan. I want to go and live somewhere else. What if I leave this town? Would you be upset, Mum?'

His mother stopped sewing at his question. She looked at her son in silence, putting the piece of cloth on her lap. Then, as if she had heard nothing, she took up her sewing again.

'I'd like to go to either Seoul or Tokyo.'

Still she made no reply.

'Can't you see how I detest this place?' Kyung-sik exclaimed in a tone expressive of his disgust, hatred and despair.

Since his father deserted his family, Kyung-sik had never, not once, expressed to anyone his opinion about his father. He kept his resentment and bitterness inside. Kyung-sik was too proud to speak of his personal problems to outsiders. He did not want to give anyone a chance to gossip about him or feel sorry for him. He could not bear to receive pity from strangers.

It was nearly three years since his father had deserted his family. Kyung-sik had been hurt so much that there seemed no possible consolation for him. Whenever he saw his mother sewing at night in order to survive, Kyung-sik's heart swelled with distress and agony, leaving a huge scar there. He found it humiliating to encounter people's sympathetic gaze on the street. He could not endure their jokes about his father's mistress, Ae-kyung, and her debauched life style.

'I want to study in a big city, Mother,' Kyung-sik sighed, trying to control his tears. 'I'll send for you as soon as I become successful. I promise, mother.'

Kyung-sik felt as though something deep inside him was about to explode. Something that had been kept inside him so patiently for so long finally burst out as he eagerly disclosed his plans and dreams to his mother.

After Hisaya's disappearance, several women had come to see Kyung-sik's mother to give her the news. Some came out of curiousity, hoping to evoke some response from Kyung-sik's mother. Some unwittingly humiliated and hurt Kyung-sik and his mother with their careless remarks.

'That bitch Ae-kyung is a treacherous woman,' one woman sneered. 'Even when she heard about her son's disappearance, she didn't bat an eyelid. She didn't show any emotion, just went on putting on her make-up. Isn't she a bitch?'

'She's not even human,' another said in disgust. 'I'm sure Kyung-sik's father must be fed up with her by now. You wait and see. He'll come back to you very soon!'

Kyung-sik and his mother had never expressed to anyone, never even hinted to each other, how desperately they longed for his father to come back home. Not even once had they showed how eagerly they awaited his return. Yet they were both of them yearning for him to come home from the bottom of their hearts. Their longing was so profound and desperate that it needed to be treated with concern, compassion and respect, instead of being just a matter of idle gossip.

People took every opportunity to talk about the affair – they would ask how in the world his father could find it in his heart to leave his wife and family for such a cold-blooded bitch as Ae-kyung. They loved to dwell on how his father had lost himself in alcohol and sex and how he worshipped Ae-kyung, They despised him for not being able to control himself and falling in love with such a notorious prostitute.

Kyung-sik loathed the gossips, his father and Ae-kyung. He had finally lost faith in the virtue of being patient. He could no longer keep bottled up in his heart all the misery he shared with his mother. His heart was so swollen with grief that it was about to burst. And so Kyung-sik felt it was time to leave this shameful, heart-breaking town and finally found the courage to tell his mother his plans.

'No. You're not going anywhere,' his mother finally replied. Her usually colourless tone of voice was quite different; it was firm and stern, not hesitant or trembling but determined and resolved, conveying more strength than simple dissent. Amazed and bitterly disappointed, Kyung-sik stared at his mother.

Just then, the neighbour's wall clock announced that it was one o'clock in the morning. The significance of this time had been imprinted on his heart for a long time. His mother used to sit up every night until one o'clock, waiting for his father and hoping for his return. Back when she had hope for her husband, Kyung-sik's mother did not need to take in sewing for a living. She used to sit up, motionless like a wooden doll, waiting, and even after he deserted her, still she would wait up for her husband night after night, still hoping and wishing for his return. Since she never went to bed until after one in the morning, it had become Kyung-sik's habit as well.

Kyung-sik used to pretend to be asleep whenever the neighbour's clock struck one. Whenever he heard the clock, his heart sank, and he became engulfed by melancholy and depression.

Everywhere was still now; the sound of fulling had died away for some time. Only a cricket's soft chirping from under the wooden floor penetrated the stillness of the night. Suddenly, heavy footsteps were heard outside the closed window. Kyung-sik to assumed that it was some playboy hastening home. But the footsteps had halted, right on the terrace stones in the front courtyard. Before he could conjecture further, the door was flung open. Someone tall, in his spring coat and a felt hat, looked inside awkwardly. The mysterious man was Kyung-sik's father. Mr Yoon.

Kyung-sik and his mother were so shocked to see him that they almost screamed. Since his father abandoned his family, Kyung-sik had not once even met him in the street. Somehow his father seemed taller than he remembered. Kyung-sik noticed that his father reeked of uncleanliness and seemed coarsened by his life style. Mr Yoon's face was flushed from a long walk in the cold air. He wore a rough, menacing expression on his face, as if he were about to start shouting. Kyung-sik's mother got to her feet and stood in a daze. She appeared to be apprehensive, even terrified by her husband's dream-like arrival.

'Do you mind if I come inside?' Mr Yoon asked hesitantly. He had finally come to ask forgiveness for his sins. He had finally come back to his wife and son. Repenting of his iniquities, Mr Yoon had come home to be with them, not to hurt them as Kyung-sik and his mother had feared.

'Please forgive me,' Mr Yoon apologized, lowering his head. 'I'm sorry I have hurt you so much.'

At her husband's true repentance, she wept unceasingly. Even in the presence of her son, she could not stop crying, releasing all her pent-up hurt feelings in her warm tears. Of course she forgave him. She welcomed him back with open arms, letting bygones be bygones. For her a miracle had occurred – her husband had finally come home.

Her happiness, however, did not last long. After staying home for five weeks, Mr Yoon left his family once again. He rushed back to his mistress Ae-kyung, knelt down and begged her forgiveness. He wept bitterly and begged her to have him back. He confessed that he had been jealous, he admitted how wrong he had been to suspect her love for him, he cried that he was terribly sorry to have doubted her and begged her to love him again, all the time weeping and clinging to her skirt. He had not returned empty-handed. Without telling his family, he had taken out a loan with his house for security, and had brought the money with him.

Upon learning this incredible news, Kyung-sik's mother fainted and became seriously ill. When she recovered, Kyung-sik left town, carrying a small suitcase.

'I'll come back for you, Mother,' he said emotionally. This time his mother did not have the heart to discourage him. She gave him her blessing.

'Go wherever you must, my son.'

Kyung-sik's mother sold everything she could for money. Even though he stubbornly refused to accept the money, she insisted on giving him everything she possessed. She believed this was the only thing she could do for her son now that his father had failed them again. Giving him all her money was the least, and the last, way she could show her love for him.

With mixed emotions Kyung-sik left town, leaving his mother all alone. After sending her son away, Kyung-sik's mother left the door wide open, not caring about the gathering cold. The courtyard was painted pale blue by the moon, and the crickets were chirping in a harmonious chorus. Jade green silk, the colour enhanced by a moonbeam, covered her room floor. Previously she had pulled it out among the new materials. Now she wondered indifferently what had made her spread the silk out on the floor. 'Oh yes, I wanted to show

Kyung-sik I'd be all right after he left me,' she remembered her motive. Then she stopped thinking completely, sitting there among the silk, still and rigid as a marble statue.

*   *   *

The news of Sinn-sil's fairy-tale engagement to the son of the richest man in town stirred up great excitement in Wonjin. The rumour was confirmed when several excellent seam-stresses were asked to sew for the wedding. Kyung-sik's mother was the first to be chosen for this task as the best and most reliable seamstress in town. She was again the subject of much gossip among the village people. She remained in ignorance of the gossip. She neither knew nor cared about anything outside her own unhappy world.

3

The autumn sky was crystal clear, boldly displaying its cobalt blue. Sung-aah's father, Dr Baek, was on his way back to Wonjin from a remote country village. The typical harvest scenes of well-ripened, golden sheaves of corn in the field and busy farmers threshing their rice were rare even in the remote countryside. The land was too poor and barren to produce much of anything, and most of fields were covered with stones. The nature of the rough, uneven land symbolized the villagers' hard life.

Dr Baek could identify a few sites where people used to grow various grains and vegetables. As he walked along the country road, he enjoyed the rare opportunity to witness the colours of autumn – red and yellow leaves dancing freely on the ground, a clear, rolling stream nearby – and marvelled at nature's ceaseless wonders. The country road was bathed in morning sunlight. Dr Baek felt good in this quiet, friendly environment. It was still early.

'I love to be out in the countryside,' Dr Baek exclaimed aloud so that his companions could hear. 'I think the clean, crisp country air is good for body and mind.'

'You're right, sir,' the young clerk agreed with Dr Baek

eagerly, bending at the waist humbly, even though Dr Baek was walking ahead of him.

The clerk, in his shorts and yellow shirt, carried Dr Baek's medicine bag. Dr Baek's assistant, Mr Oh, was accompanying them along the country road.

'I really love this cool air,' Dr Baek exclaimed again.

'Sir,' the clerk called in an excited tone. 'I cannot find words to express my appreciation for your services last night. You haven't even slept; you stayed up all night to take care of the patient. Thank you very much, sir.'

'Don't mention it, my friend,' Dr Baek said kindly. 'I was only doing my job. I just did what any doctor would do, you know.'

'Well, sir, you did more than anybody else,' the clerk said sincerely. 'You came such a long distance to tend that patient. I understand the former community doctor never bothered to come even when someone begged him to. He used to show up a few days later with a detective and leave straight after a brief examination.'

The clerk turned to Mr Oh and remarked: 'Not that I blame him for not coming earlier. Who wants to see a body, anyway?' The clerk sounded as though he were apologizing. Mr Oh, whose face was covered with pimples, entirely ignored him, wanting nothing to do with such a country bumpkin.

'This is not the first time I've been to your village,' Dr Baek murmured after a short silence. 'That means you have had quite a few mishaps there.'

'I'm afraid you're right there, sir,' the clerk agreed, dropping his eyes uneasily. The clerk was not upset by what Dr Baek said, but he felt embarrassed for his village as a whole. He had to admit that, as Dr Baek remarked, there had been many violent incidents among the villagers lately. People did not hesitate to fight and do each other harm. The clerk had heard of a good many horrible injuries occurring in such fights. One man had attempted to attack another with a sickle, but was struck first with a large stone by his opponent. Bones were broken, and faces disfigured. Usually the injured would wait for their wounds to heal of their own accord. They would dress their wounds with soy bean paste, and sometimes apply heat to help them heal faster.

Unlike the other fights, however, last night's fight had had a fatal result – one dead and another critically wounded. Right after the tragedy, the tender-hearted clerk had rushed to town for Dr Baek, running all the way in his bare feet.

Dr Baek had performed an autopsy on the dead man and given emergency treatment to the badly wounded man. After rendering his medical services he could have gone back to town the same night; he could have returned home with the policeman who had accompanied him to the village. However, he decided to stay on, hoping to save his patient's life.

Dr Baek was pleased that he could inhale the cool, fresh country air; however, he was becoming overwhelmed with fatigue. He felt utterly exhausted. There was not even a donkey available for him to ride to ease his fatigue. He had no choice but to walk all the way to Wonjin. Since the previous afternoon Dr Baek had eaten nothing. However, neither hunger nor sleeplessness was the real cause of his sudden exhaustion. Some other unpleasant feeling, like an omen, loomed ever larger over him. An overwhelming sensation of sluggishness and lethargy, a piercing chill, and a feeling of dizziness that nearly made him black out – all of these familiar yet ignored symptoms of his poor health suddenly seized him, leaving him helpless and weary.

While examining the body on the stretcher last night, Dr Baek had experienced a strangely unpleasant sensation, chilling his spine. Now he recalled last night's feeling as he walked along the dusty country road. He had witnessed and treated many different, horribly mutilated bodies in his professional career; therefore, it was not the young man's battered face that upset him. Actually, Dr Baek hadn't felt well even before he left home; he suspected his lunch might have upset his stomach. Perhaps he was coming down with flu, he thought. He now felt terribly weak and tired. The mounting fatigue seemed to come from the very depths of his being.

Dr Baek was a well-built man wearing gold-rimmed glasses. He projected a professional image of cool, impersonal efficiency which had nothing to do with his true personality which was warm and friendly. He had a strong personal belief that everyone should be treated with respect and understanding and practised his beliefs in his daily activities. He was always ready to help people if he could. He understood and had compassion for people. He never showed anger, frustration, or annoyance over social injustice or brutality; he merely accepted the pattern of life and humbly lived with it.

'I understand the man who was beaten to death has no relatives whatsoever. Is it true?' Dr Baek asked gently. He was feeling better now that his dizziness had passed. As a professional man, Dr Baek had been considerably inured to his patients' physical plight, suffering and misery. Like any other doctor, he showed no emotion or sympathy when he examined or tended his patients, treating them as impersonally as if they were a form of machinery that needed repair.

'Are you referring to the dead man when you ask whether he has any relatives, sir?'

'No, I'm talking about the man who was arrested. You know, he isn't a bad looking fellow at all.'

At Dr Baek's remark, the clerk hesitated to comment on the killer, who had escaped to the mountain after his crime and later given himself up. After Dr Baek and his assistant, Mr Oh, arrived in the village, the murderer had surrendered to the policemen; they had taken him to town, his hands tied behind him with ropes.

The clerk marvelled at Dr Baek's keen observation. How in the world had he managed to find time to see the accused, anyway? He and his assistant, Mr Oh, had been busy taking care of the patient under the big lamp-lit tree near the pavilion, and had not even raised their heads while they were engaged in their medical treatment. The clerk realized Dr Baek was still waiting for an answer. It was impolite to remain silent.

'The accused is my friend, sir,' he finally replied in a tearful voice. 'The dead man was also a good friend of mine. To tell you the truth, sir, the one whose life you just saved this morning is the luckiest of all.

'The dead friend had just returned home from another city to find out about his wife's unfaithfulness. His wife was having an affair with the man whom you saved this morning. My friend who tried to prevent them from fighting accidentally killed the innocent party, sir. It was an accident, a shameful accident.'

'Oh, I see,' Dr Baek responded briefly, not asking any further questions. It was one of those pathetic affairs that frequently stirred up the villages in the remote, poor

countryside. The causes of murder were nearly always the same
– tragic squabbles between an incompatible mother-in-law and
her daughter-in-law or brutal fights after gambling parties.
However, this incident was more tragic than usual. Innocent
young men got involved: the result was death. Dr Baek felt
full of regret that such an unnecessary tragedy had to happen.

'What a shame,' he said emotionally. 'It certainly is a
shame.'

The clerk sniffed at Dr Baek's statement as if he were trying
not to cry.

'Do you go to work in town every day?' Dr Baek changed
the subject tactfully. 'It is quite a distance, you know.'

'Yes, sir,' the clerk agreed, shifting the doctor's bag as if it
were something very precious.

'Why don't you go home now?' Dr Baek suggested. 'I think
we can manage from here. This road looks familiar. Go on
home now.'

'I don't mind, sir,' the clerk said.

'Mr Oh, why don't you carry the bag now?' Dr Baek asked.
'I'm sure our friend is worn out.'

'Please, sir,' the clerk insisted, 'I really don't mind walking
with you.'

Finally, Dr Baek, Mr Oh, and the town clerk reached a
small earthen bridge. Good-sized carp were swimming freely
in the clear brook under the bridge. Dr Baek turned his head
indicating his intention to say something. At the corner of his
mouth, a warm, gentle smile began to form. Suddenly, his face
turned chalk pale, and he slumped to the ground.

'Sir!' Mr Oh and the clerk tried to support Dr Baek who had
already lost all his energy and strength, bending his neck
backward. Mr Oh and the clerk took it in turns to carry Dr
Baek on their backs to the country bus station. Fortunately, a
truck stopped for them. The truck driver had recognized Dr
Baek and offered to take him to the state hospital in a
neighbouring city.

Even though the truck driver had an emergency task in the
opposite direction from the hospital, he was glad to lend a
hand, for he remembered how Dr Baek had helped his son
some winters back. The driver's son was his only child and
consequently, when he had a convulsion, the driver was
frantic. He ran all the way to Dr Baek's office to seek his

medical attention. Of course, Dr Baek responded without hesitation and the child was saved.

When he was admitted to the emergency room at the state hospital, Dr Baek was struggling for his life. His pulse was weak but still showed signs of life. Before Dr Baek was put under intensive care, he had been given an injection by Mr Oh, once at the country bus station and once in the truck. Unlike the clerk who was in a state of helpless shock, Mr Oh had the sense to try to take care of Dr Baek.

Despite all of the medical care, however, Dr Baek passed away after remaining unconscious for a day and a half, desperately fighting for his breath. His sudden death was beyond description. People were confounded with astonishment at the news. The cause of his death was uncertain – the hospital authorities tried to explain it in many different ways. What was the point of knowing the cause of death, anyway? The only thing that mattered was the cold, harsh reality – Dr Baek was gone.

The world Dr Baek had created was peaceful, warm and secure. He touched everyone with his special care, affection and concern, affecting so many others directly or indirectly. Now his world, which used to be so friendly and close, was shattered, without any consideration for his family. Dr Baek had been a solid foundation, a root and cornerstone in the world for his patients as well as his family.

Death is an unavoidable and universal phenomenon. No one can control, plan for, or compensate for it; it is an understood, expected event of life, yet, it is never fully welcomed or accepted. From the beginning it has been a mystery, and as long as humanity endures, the mystery of death will remain.

4

The school children stood in a row in the playground. The harsh, cold wind blew ceaselessly, swaying the girls' thin skirts at will and turning their cheeks blue as if they had been bruised. They bent their back and knees slightly in an attempt to escape from the brutal lash of the wind. The boys clenched their fists tightly, half-standing, half-bending. The principal's speech seemed endless. Even when he had finished, there would still be the assistant-principal's wearisome instructions. Whenever there was a school gathering or ceremony, the children were obliged to endure this ritual – first the principal's talk, and then the assistant-principal's boring admonitions. Most of the children did not even understand the meaning of it all, nor did they know why they were forced to endure this physical discomfort, bending their backs back and forth to gain temporary relief from the piercing wind. Usually they had to stand still in the school yard for half an hour or more.

The angry sky was blanketed by dark grey clouds. Sand driven by the fierce wind savagely attacked the children's legs, hands, and faces. Deliberately, Young-sil moved her entire body, lifting her feet and putting them down on the ground. She speeded up her exercise; she was trembling violently like a malaria patient. The teachers who were standing in a line on the elevated area occasionally glared at Young-sil; some looked ready to dash to her any minute in anger and disgust. However, their menacing looks did not bother her. She completely ignored them.

Young-sil could not help feeling resentful, standing there in the open school yard in the piercing cold wind. She had tried not to let herself be affected by the weather, yet she could not help rebelling against the stubborn, harsh wind that whipped her so mercilessly and the long-winded principal. He looked like an idiot. Why must he talk so long, wasting everybody's time? She could not stand this stupidity any longer. Her lips quivered from the relentless wind and her whole body shook. She wished it was time for them to sing.

In despair, Young-sil gazed at the dreary sky, moving her head to and fro freely. Gloomy clouds festooned the sky, soon scattered by the ferocious wind. Watching the sky, Young-sil was suddenly gripped with a strange sensation. Abruptly, she stopped moving; a feeling as mournful and heavy as the leaden grey sky slowly flowed over her from the depths of her inner soul. 'What can it be?' Young-sil wondered frantically. 'What makes me feel so sad and heavy-hearted?' she asked herself over and over again.

Just as the time at last came for the school children to bow deeply, nearly touching their toes, Young-sil remembered why she felt overpowered with grief. It was because of Sung-aah and her family – ever since Dr Baek's unforeseen death they had been on her mind. She found it hard to accept his death. Had he really passed away? Could it really happen like that? How could it be justified, for Sung-aah and her family's happiness to be so brutally shattered?

Dr Baek's sudden death was so shocking that in spite of her apparent insensitivity, Young-sil's heart was heavy with sadness and a sense of loss.

Obeying the teacher's command, the children bowed repeatedly. Lost in her unfathomable thoughts, Young-sil stood straight, licking her finger. She was still thinking of Dr Baek's death and its tragic aftermath. Since he was dead, Sung-aah's mother would not smile as sweetly as she used to; Sung-aah's warm-hearted grandmother would no longer pass out fresh fruit or biscuits to children as she used to. The storyteller, Koo-bae's grandfather, would not visit Sung-aah's house any more. Worst of all, Sung-aah would not play the organ.

Young-sil vividly recalled the melodious sound of the electric organ as if the trailing notes still lingered in her ears. Everything bright, safe, and secure in Sung-aah's household had disappeared with the death of Dr Baek. Everything was finished for them. Even though Young-sil believed she could never enjoy such security or well-being in their own house, she was happy merely to observe them enjoying their lives. She loved to visit Sung-aah's house. The knowledge that Sung-aah and her family were well-to-do and secure in every way, used to give Young-sil a kind of emotional security. Now it had all vanished like bubbles bursting. Such profound happiness and security should not be destroyed so suddenly.

Sung-aah had not attended school this morning. She had been absent for a few days. As a matter of fact, Dr Baek's funeral had been held just the day before. Young-sil pictured Sung-aah's bleak house that was now as cold and silent as a tomb. The cold wind continued to harass Young-sil and the other children in the playground. Suddenly, her misery was too much for her. She burst into tears that spilled on the ground.

After the ceremony, celebrating some Japanese festival day, a vindictive teacher ordered Young-sil to stand in the middle of the school yard as a punishment for her misconduct during the ceremony. The reason for her punishment was ridiculous: she wept while the other children sang in chorus, hiding her eyes with cupped hands. She had also blown her nose out loud on her skirt hem just when the principal, in his white gloves, carried the Japanese emperor's portrait. Her heart was so swollen with grief that she did not even notice the penetrating cold any more. All she knew was that everything was finished and broken – everything bright and happy had disappeared with the death of Dr Baek.

Young-sil was also suffering severely from the acute pain of loneliness and a feeling of being left out, especially when she thought about Dr Baek's unexpected death. She was not one of the family, yet a strong sense of loss and grief gripped her. In deep sorrow, she looked at her feet blankly and wept again. Warm tears streamed down her cheeks.

After a good while remaining in the same posture, Young-sil lifted her head slowly and looked at the school building. The two-storey, narrow, drab brick building met her inattentive eyes. The countless windows of the teachers' room wore a dead look, even though there must have been quite a few teachers inside. Judging from the expressionless windows, no one seemed to be bothering to check on her.

She decided to leave the school yard, disobeying the teacher's instructions. She walked slowly towards the school entrance, in complete defiance of orders, and with no feeling of guilt. Even though she was a little nervous about the possibility of a sterner punishment tomorrow by the same teacher, who might remember her face, it really did not matter to her all that much. Nothing seemed important in her present frame of mind.

Young-sil never worried about consequences. She simply acted as her emotions dictated, without thought for the consequences. Nothing came between her feelings and her actions; not even shame or common sense could change her mind once she had decided to do something.

In reality, she knew she would be all right. No one, not even that strict teacher, could bother her. Perhaps she was too shameless in some matters; perhaps she took some things too lightly. Yet she had the instinct to recognize when something was dangerous or safe, to her advantage or disadvantage. At times, she would admit, she had been mean, base and cheap in handling matters. Her behaviour was ruled by her emotions – whenever she thought something was profitable, she would act accordingly, without feeling shame or guilt. She was often overwhelmed by certain, intense feelings, surging up from the depths of her innermost soul. She could not describe exactly her own emotional state, yet she always responded to her feelings.

Young-sil had made it her business to visit Sung-aah daily. After supper she would descend the hill and head for Sung-aah's house. On the way she had to pass the hut of the pathetic old man who used to complain how he had been mistreated by his own children. He would shake his fist upward to the sky, his torn shirt sleeve flapping in the air whenever he raised his arm.

After the funeral, Sung-aah's house had been as quiet as the deep sea. The entrance to Dr Baek's clinic was locked; the grief-stricken Mr Oh, Dr Baek's assistant, kept to his room next to the dispensary. For the first few days Sung-aah's family had been extremely sensitive to Young-sil's visits. Whenever she was with them, they would burst into sobs as if they had only been awaiting Young-sil to initiate the family mourning. As soon as she saw Sung-aah and her family, Young-sil's eyes would automatically well up with tears. Her lips trembled slightly, as she tried not to cry aloud. No one cried audibly except Young-sil, who could not control herself.

For the first time in her life, Young-sil felt with a pang how painful it is to swallow tears. She realized what unfathomable grief Sung-aah's family must be suffering in their silent weeping. However, as the days passed, their weeping became somewhat reduced in frequency. The intensity of pain and sorrow had begun to lessen. Sung-aah's family looked forward to Young-sil's visits. As though crying was the only way to relieve their pain and anxiety, they were in the desperate stage of grasping at any temporary comfort. They seemed to find solace in their silent sobbing and Young-sil's honest, open tears. Even Sung-aah's mother and grandmother seemed to share Sung-aah's dependence on Young-sil as a comforter.

The black-ribboned floral wreath that decorated the corner of the front courtyard, during the mourning period, had gone. The main hall, which used to be partly furnished with familiar medical equipment, was also completely cleared. The empty courtyard and the main hall were filled instead with a strange, dreadful sense of absolute loss. The house was pervaded with the mysterious, frightening scent of ceaselessly burning incense. Several people, including the storytelling old man, came to express their condolences. After they left, Sung-aah's family had to face the enormous emptiness and loneliness anew. And so they welcomed the faithful visits of Young-sil, who seemed to share their sorrow and was willing to spend long lonely evenings with them. Sung-aah's family had become exceptionally sensitive in their tragic situation. They were easily hurt by insignificant matters. They had become vulnerable in their distress.

In this phenomenon of family suffering, Young-sil had become totally involved in her friend's distress. It was almost as if Young-sil had become part of Sung-aah's family.

Then one day Young-sil's faithful devotion in calling on her friend's family abruptly ceased. There was no particular reason or explanation for this. It had nothing to do with Sung-aah's family or any change in Sung-aah's household. She just didn't want to see them any more. Her attention swung away from their sorrow to her sister's approaching wedding. Presents were arriving and preparations were occupying the household.

One morning Young-sil came into a room near the kitchen. A pile of many different cushions, richly and tastefully embroidered pillow cases, and fragments of fine fabrics caught her eye. She also found an almost completed hand-made blanket cover meticulously trimmed with lace; a lace cover for the mirror, and a vase mat in a large box by the stack of cushions and pillow cases. These fine, delicate things immediately entranced her.

'Oh, my word, look at all these beautiful things,' she exclaimed excitedly. Her sister, Sinn-sil, touched her bridal things without showing any emotion. Her face wore a dream-like, trouble-free, composed expression. Young-sil's mother, also quiet by nature, stood up and sat down repeatedly in an excited and urgent manner. Her situation had turned full circle. Once a professional seamstress, now she found herself asking people to sew for her. That meant she had to examine carefully all the work other seamstresses had done for her. She took no pleasure in urging them to hurry their work, especially when she had to ask them to mend unsatisfactory work done

101

in haste. She was becoming exhausted by these tiresome preparations for her daughter's marriage.

Sinn-sil's girlfriends came in groups to see her every day. They were old enough to be brides themselves. As they walked swiftly, their braided hair moved to and fro. One of the girls braided her hair under the ear very tightly while her short hair was awkwardly tied behind; another tied her long hair very loosely, letting it flow down to her plump shoulders and breasts.

'My goodness gracious! What in the world are these?' one girl exclaimed, excitedly.

'Yes, Sinn-sil, what are these?' the other joined in eagerly. Sinn-sil's friends seemed engrossed in the fine, beautiful fabrics that had been brought for her marriage. Some could not hide their chagrin, springing from their obvious jealousy and envy of Sinn-sil's good fortune; others simply giggled foolishly.

Sinn-sil's father, Mr Shin, had remained in his room all day while the mood of the forthcoming wedding heightened. Her friends were accustomed to Sinn-sil's father, who used to glare at them whenever they ventured into the house. Looking annoyed and vexed, he would rush out of his room to scare them away. Sinn-sil's friends, dismayed at her father's behaviour, did not dare to come and see Sinn-sill as often as they would have liked. Now, her father stayed in his room, not being bothered at all. Mr Shin's uncomfortable silence did not necessarily mean that he disapproved of his daughter's marriage to the son of the wealthiest family in town. He had not revealed his feelings about the wedding one way or the other. Nevertheless, he must have consented to give his daughter away to the rich family; otherwise, the wedding preparations could not have been made in his house. An outsider could not have guessed or imagined that Mr Shin might have caused problems. People would automatically have believed that it would have been Mr Chang's family who might have made things difficult.

Whenever Sinn-sil's friends burst out in hearty laughter or fell into ecstasies over fine material, her mother instinctively cast worried, frightened glances in the direction of Mr Shin's tightly closed door.

As the days passed fine, fancy gifts had accumulated for

Sinn-sil's wedding. The quantity of the gifts was so great that there was nowhere to show them properly. They were scattered here and there throughout the entire house. Sinn-sil had made a modern frame for the map of the Korean peninsula, divided into its thirteen provinces; it was beautifully embroidered with thirteen roses of Sharon. She had also made an embroidered silk money pouch and spoon case. However, her work was put aside; the room was filled with shiny, glossy, fancy stuff brought directly from Seoul. A shiny quilt cover, silverware, a mirror and a brass basin were among the many gifts Sinn-sil had received from her future-in-laws. She had also received a handsome purse and parasol sent from Tokyo by her fiancé, Soo-chul Chang.

When a diamond ring, a white gold bracelet and a jade hairpin arrived for Sinn-sil, Young-sil's bursting excitement reached a climax. From outside she ran into the room, still carrying one shoe, and sat down on the reed mat.

'Let me see!' she cried 'Is there some more or is this everything?' Young-sil threw her boots down on to the floor and grabbed the jewellery in her grimy hands. She chattered excitedly as if she didn't know what she was saying. Her mother nodded her head deeply as if she were well-pleased with the fine jewellery.

'I was told more is coming,' her mother replied in satisfaction. 'A pearl ring and some gold buttons are coming.' Young-sil's mother generally stayed neutral, rarely expressing her opinion in any circumstances. But this time she responded eagerly without reservation.

'Pearl ring? Did you say pearl?' Young-sil asked eagerly. At the mention of a pearl, Young-sil's thoughts flew to the pearly shade on the lamp that had been given to Sung-aah by her secret admirer Chang-kyu sometime ago.

'Pearl!' Young-sil exclaimed again. 'My dear sister, will you let me keep it when you receive it? You have so many nice things already. Please let me have the pearl ring!'

'Are you out of your mind, girl?' her mother scolded, cuffing her head lightly. 'Give those to me. You might spoil them with your dirty hands!' Her mother spoke sternly as she tried to take them away from Young-sil.

'Please, mother, let me look at them,' Young-sil pleaded, turning her back. 'I only want to examine them without

103

rushing.' She put all the jewellery in her grubby skirt and carefully picked up each one and looked at it against the sunlight. The hem of her discoloured skirt was so worn that the threads hung loose like a spider's web.

'How much do you think these jewels would be worth altogether, Mother?'

'You have no business to ask that, child. Let me have them back right away.'

'What fine thing these are! I just can't get over what wonderful, beautiful stones they are – I'm so impressed! The diamond ring fits the middle finger; the pearl ring the index finger; the gold ring the third finger . . .'

'You'd better give them back to me, my girl, and I mean it.'

'Wait a second, Mother. I just want to look at them once more. I won't be long I promise.' Young-sil's tongue clacked on and on. At her stubbornness, her mother dropped her hands as if she had given up on her daughter. Against her will she had to wait until her daughter had finished admiring the jewellery.

$$*\qquad *\qquad *$$

As soon as the last class was over, Young-sil rushed to the playground, dragging her damaged rubber shoes. She could not wait to tell her friend Soon-hee all about Sinn-sil's latest presents. Her mind was full the wonderful, delightful things happening to her sister.

'Soon-hee!' Young-sil called her name, panting heavily in excitement. Soon-hee, who had been walking ahead of Young-sil, stopped and turned her head. Soon-hee could not be sure of Young-sil's intention being so eager and friendly after such a long period of indifference and aloofness towards her. In this doubtful mood, Soon-hee stood still and cast an uncertain glance towards Young-sil.

'Please listen to me,' Young-sil put her arm round Soon-hee's shoulders in the old easy way. Young-sil was already intoxicated with the approaching joy and happiness that she was going to share with her friend. She beamed all over her face as she walked along, her arm round Soon-hee's shoulders. As she felt the familiar intimacy from the weight and warmth of Young-sil's body, Soon-hee's resentment at being ignored and neglected melted instantly. She was overwhelmed with delight at her friend's renewal of their friendship. Without realizing it, Soon-hee found herself caught up in Young-sil's unspoken excitement that had to be shared somehow.

'What's up, my friend?' Soon-hee asked with interest.

Young-sil began to pour out a stream of chatter about her sister's forthcoming wedding. As she told her story with many a touch of exaggeration and many a lavish detail, her descriptions became colourful, joyful and beautiful like sparkling evening stars. As Young-sil and Soon-hee passed by the front gate of the school, they saw Sung-aah standing by the gate. Young-sil guested that Sung-aah had been waiting there for her. Sung-aah tried to smile at Young-sil, but Young-sil passed her by, completely ignoring her. She instinctively knew that Sung-aah was less likely to be impressed by her tales. She did not want to spoil her own mood by worrying about more than one listener at a time.

She noticed the hurt expression on Sung-aah's face, but decided not to dwell on it.

'Did you know my sister had received many fine gifts from the groom?' Young-sil boasted, adding that it was rather difficult to remember everything.

As she tried to describe her sister's fine jewellery, she became more and more excited. She exaggerated how precious the stones were, what beautiful shapes and forms they had, and how many other expensive things her sister had received. Her extensive, impressive description of the jewellery reminded Soon-hee of the brilliant colours and beautiful designs of the jewellery proudly displayed in the window of the jeweller's down town.

Young-sil was so rapt in ecstasy that she had entirely forgotten about Sung-aah and her family's tragedy even though not long ago she was ready to spend the rest of her life with them, sharing their grief. Although Young-sil knew how much they needed her company, her heart had turned in a different direction, completely forsaking their silent cries.

Young-sil felt so happy that she could almost fly into the sky in her present mood. Why could not life always be this good and delicious, she thought. She could not help looking down on those who were underprivileged and had nothing to rejoice about. Young-sil regarded them as insignificant, even worthless. Everybody should live in a mansion in order to enjoy what life is really like, Young-sil concluded. Her heart was swollen with pride and anticipation as she thought of an easy life style like that of the wealthiest man, Mr Daal-soo Chang.

Intoxicated with glee, Young-sil told Soon-hee that her family would soon be moving to a comfortable, big, nice house. As it was, she added, each room in her house was cluttered with fragments of silk. However, her exaggerated, bragging claims were contradicted by her outward appearance. Her long skirt was so old and worn-out that its hem hung loose like a spider's web, yet she appeared embarrassingly unaware of it. In essence, Young-sil lacked sensitivity. Whenever she was absorbed in her own interests, she paid no attention to mundane details. Her enthusiasms were infectious. With her animated descriptions she could inspire other people to share her excitement.

Her friend Soon-hee was helplessly captivated by Young-sil's enthralling story; and in her blissful mood, she found herself trying to picture all those splendid, gorgeous jewels in her mind too.

Soon-hee, the daughter of the fire chief, was simple and easy to please. Young-sil soon got tired of her company. She found it no fun to be with Soon-hee for very long. Hoping to relieve her boredom, Young-sil tried to make friends with Sung-aah again.

As she recalled the past, Young-sil was overcome with yearning for her old friend and her friendship. In this softened mood, Young-sil sent a friendly glance to Sung-aah; however, Sung-aah entirely ignored Young-sil's attention and appeared to be stern and aloof. Young-sil, who was generally stubborn and not easily discouraged, found Sung-aah's cold response difficult to accept, but she was obliged to admit defeat.

Unlike her other friends, Sung-aah had never, not even once, complied with Young-sil's whims. She had never forsaken her pride in order to please Young-sil. Even though they had been very good friends, Young-sil was compelled to respect Sung-aah; she realized her friend was not easily manipulated. During their friendship only once did Young-sil and Sung-aah really share their feelings and that was after Sung-aah's father died. Young-sil and Sung-aah became very close then. Young-sil felt she had become part of Sung-aah's family, sharing their sorrow and loneliness. Dr Baek's death allowed them to become one, understanding each other. It was not, of course, Sung-aah who initiated this close relationship; it was Young-sil.

Now Young-sil recognized that Sung-aah was not the type to be easily impressed or influenced by anyone. She admired her for it. Indeed, the more Sung-aah ignored her, the more Young-sil became drawn to her former friend.

During class hours, Young-sil could not concentrate on her studies. Her mind wandered far away from the classroom. Secretly, she studied Sung-aah's expression whenever she could. Sometimes she managed to turn her upper body and stare at her friend for a while, hoping to gain her attention. Her eyes flashed messages of sympathy, apology, and appeal. Her obvious attempts to be noticed appeared ridiculous. Young-sil did not care one way or the other how she appeared to others. The only thing she wanted was to be acknowledged by Sung-aah. However, Sung-aah did not even raise her eyebrows, maintaining an expression of blank indifference on her face.

Young-sil was deeply disappointed. She hated herself, regretting her own mistake. She blamed herself for neglecting Sung-aah for so long. Yet she could not admit what she had done to make her friend so upset. In her own mind she had done nothing so wrong as to cause this friction between them. Neither of them had sought friendship in the first place. Young-sil had never asked for Sung-aah's friendship; and by the same token, Sung-aah had never refused to be her friend. Until now.

As Young-sil meditated on her friendship with Sung-aah, she became more confused. She could not see a way to solve this problem. The only thing she could be sure of was that Sung-aah was very angry with her, and was strongly resisting Young-sil's overtures of friendship.

During break Young-sil walked over to where she could see Sung-aah in the hope of being reconciled with her. Whenever Young-sil's eyes met Sung-aah's, she made a point of wearing a very friendly expression without reserve. She was accustomed to being accepted by her friends when she showed them warmth and friendliness. However, Sung-aah was an exception; she turned her face deliberately so as not to meet Young-sil's imploring eyes, and her facial expression, cold and indifferent, did not change. Young-sil realized she had lost the chance to make it up with her friend. There was no way for her to gain Sung-aah's lost friendship. She bitterly regretted her careless, tactless behaviour towards her friend; she had never experienced such pain as she was now feeling because of her rejection by Sung-aah. Full of self-blame and remorse, Young-sil walked home alone.

Soon-hee had been absent for a few days now. There had been rumours that Soon-hee was unwell; Young-sil had also heard that something unpleasant had happened to her. In general, Young-sil did not find Soon-hee important enough. Soon-hee was too easily impressed and influenced. Soon-hee laughed whenever Young-sil laughed; it was only too easy to please her with her whims and caprices. Young-sil preferred those with more strength of character.

5

It had been chilly and dreary for several days; it was hard to tell whether it was autumn or winter. The gloomy sky was thickly blanketed by large grey clouds. Even though it looked ready to snow any minute, the sky stubbornly maintained its grim appearance without any significant change. Once it started to snow, the street would be covered nearly six feet deep in one day. Everything would be frozen instantly at the touch of the snow fairy. Witnessing these symptoms of nature, people would accept the advent of harsh, cold winter on their doorsteps.

The mood outdoors was uneasy, restless as if something disastrous were waiting to happen soon. The air felt sticky and heavy; yet it was strangely clam. The sea became restless and harsh, roaring ceaselessly. The wind carried the ferocious sound of the angry sea into every corner of the streets.

Young-sil was standing inside the Chinese store. It was dark and gloomy, and the desk and ceiling in the store could be seen only dimly under the pale lamplight. The dark and dusty top shelves were almost empty; the store owner kept taking fine silks from the bottom shelves and proudly displaying his merchandise. The way he showed his silk to her mother reminded Young-sil of a Chinese magician with long finger nails. It seemed to her as though he was about to perform his magic, wearing a black round cap with a top knot on top of his head.

As he handled the shiny, rich fabric, it made a strong crumpling sound. It was so thick that it could not possibly be measured by any ordinary yardstick. The silk was measured by an especially long, narrow piece of wood which had been marked with a sharp knife for measurement.

'How do you like this? This is very good material, you know,' the Chinese merchant said. He pulled out another piece of silk and began to spread it out for Young-sil's mother's inspection. She looked very serious, scrutinizing the material. She crumpled it and wrinkled it and looked intently at the material against the dim light coming through the small window.

'It's an excellent item. It is quite expensive but it's worth it,' the Chinese merchant said in his strange accent.

Young-sil's mother swallowed deeply and appeared to be deep in thought. After her meditation, she asked the Chinese merchant to cut a portion in a sullen tone of voice. Young-sil was still wearing the long, worn-out, patched skirt. Her mother was so busy preparing for Sinn-sil's wedding that she had no time for her younger daughter. It had been so busy and hectic lately that sometimes Young-sil had missed meals. Frequently, she had been slapped by her mother for being a nuisance around the house. He mother had been extremely nervous and tense ever since the announcement of her elder daughter's marriage. Young-sil did not mind being treated like this at all; she did not care one way or the other but continued to go her own way, as usual.

When she overheard her mother's remark about going to a Chinese store to buy additional fabric, without a second thought Young-sil had run outside in front of her mother. For quite some time, she had wanted to see the Chinese store for herself. The main door of the store was always shut, not letting in much light. It always seemed dull and dark. The Chinese characters on the narrow, hanging signboard were picked out in gold paint. The bottom of the signboard was also decorated with a piece of red cloth that swayed about freely.

A lark could be seen in its cage outside the store during the summer months. Young-sil pictured the store as a spooky and terrible place to go. She believed all Chinese people were magicians. She used to hear very fascinating stories about Chinese magicians. Once she heard about a young girl whose neck was cut by a sharp scimitar bearing the figure of a blue dragon and how a red peony blossom sprang from her blood. Another time she heard the story of a man who picked up a torch lit with fire and put it in his mouth. After he had swallowed the fire, people could see an endless thread emanating from the man's mouth just as if it had been spun by a silk worm.

Recalling these captivating stories about Chinese magicians, Young-sil fixed her eyes on the long-nailed Chinese merchant. She nearly held her breath, expecting him to perform some kind of magic in front of her eyes. Was he going to begin an act that might arouse her sensations and even fear? Her imagination ran wild.

The inside door opened gently and a middle-aged woman with bound feet, carrying a child appeared from within. The child was a sweet little boy whose face had the soft texture of a round white rice cake. His clothes were of a shiny gold colour; his head was completely shaved except on the very top where hair was left in the shape of a small square. His shaven head resembled a round, white, well-shaped onion. Young-sil stared at the little boy, wondering whether he could be a product of Chinese magic himself. Young-sil could not help adoring him. He was wearing beautifuly embroidered red silk shoes.

'Goodness gracious, what a darling baby you are!' Young-sil exclaimed emotionally. Then she carefully touched the baby's soft, plump cheek as if she could not resist her urge to do so. As the little Chinese baby boy moved his little, round hand, his gold bracelet with tiny bells made a pleasing sound. His mother said something gleefully, laughing softly.

Young-sil's mother took the cloth wrapper in her arms and hastily left the store. At her mother's abrupt departure, Young-sil ran after her mother hurriedly.

'What a precious baby he is! I think he is so sweet,' she exclaimed. Her mother remained silent, preoccupied.

'When I grow up, I'll have a fine baby just like him – cute and handsome. I'll keep him always neat and nice so everybody can't help but admire him.'

110

Her mother still paid no attention to Young-sil's excited chatter.

'Mother, dear, how is it you don't know how to appreciate the finer things in life?'

Her mother went on walking, making no comment whatsoever.

'I feel sorry for you, mother.'

Abruptly Young-sil stopped chattering as she spotted Soon-hee's father, Mr Choi, the former fire chief, walking ahead of them, slowly with pride and dignity. A few months earlier, Mr Choi had been dismissed from his post, yet he still wore his uniform and matching cap. His gait was deliberate and his posture was straight and stern.

Young-sil's mother quickened her steps towards her house, passing Mr Choi. Young-sil, on the contrary, slowed down and followed Mr Choi. She was thinking of one particular incident that happened not long ago. After he was officially dismissed from his job, Mr Choi went on going to his office and trying to take care of his business. This behaviour caused a great deal of confusion and commotion in the fire station. Mr Choi could not understand the meaning of his dismissal. No one, in fact, had been able to make him understand that he was no longer the fire chief.

Even though Mr Choi had already moved out of the station (he and his daughter used to live in a room adjacent to his office), he went to the office every single morning. His expression was always serious and dignified. The fire station staff used to watch for him and block the way to the office. Sometimes they had to pull him out of the office. Their efforts to keep him out of the office had been moderately successful. The new fire chief had been able to do his job without much difficulty. However, one day Mr Choi managed to sneak into the office and go through all the official documents. In addition, he put his personal stamp on each paper for final approval.

Mr Choi mumbled frequently as he walked. Suddenly he halted and put his hand into his inside breast pocket that was trimmed with fine gold cord. He took out a handful of his business cards from his inner pocket and examined them carefully for a good while. He continued to climb the hilly road until he reached Sung-aah's house, and then he turned round. He slowly descended the hilly road and continued in the direction leading to the marketplace.

Young-sil still followed Mr Choi, preoccupied with thoughts about Sung-aah and Soon-hee. Their world was so completely different from her own. Young-sil realized she had nothing in common with either of them. Their lives seemed to be intense, abnormal, fraught with tragedy. Compared with them, Young-sil found her own life style delightful. She felt as if she were floating on air. As she thought of her friends, she was seized with a strong urge to lead a normal life, a real life, even if it did have problems.

For the second time, Mr Choi climbed the hilly road and stopped near Sung-aah's house. Then he turned round and walked down again. This time Young-sil did not follow him. She stood on the pavement facing Sung-aah's house, looking at the triangular roof above the entrance hall. She remained silent for a long time. She had not the courage to visit Sung-aah and her family. That was something that was beyond even her boldness and brashness. Something that she could not explain restrained her from entering Sung-aah's house.

Sung-aah's family had had to endure another ordeal before they were able to recover from their shocking family tragedy. This newly developed crisis was nothing compared with Dr Baek's death, yet it was another small tragedy for Sung-aah's family.

Sung-aah's widowed mother was still young and inexperienced; Sung-aah was extremely sensitive. When the shadow of fear and uncertainty about their future fell over them, they were at a loss to know what to do. They did not know how they were to overcome their overwhelming problems.

Dr Baek's assistant, Mr Oh, was moody by nature. He was an orphan who had experienced many hardships during his childhood. He had no particular place to stay, so he moved about constantly in order to stay alive. Because of his predicament, Dr Baek used to feel sorry for Mr Oh, and showed his compassion by taking him in and making him his personal assistant.

Since Dr Baek's death, Mr Oh had been overwhelmed by grief and sorrow, secluding himself from the world. At first, Sung-aah's family did not pay much attention to his mournful silence. However, as the days went by, his sorrow became a

burden to Sung-aah's family, who also desperately needed
something or someone to lean on. Sung-aah's mother was
particularly disturbed by Mr Oh's mourning for her husband.
One evening the concerned Mrs Baek called on Mr Oh and
explained: 'I understand how you must feel, Mr Oh. Dr
Baek's death was a great shock for all of us. He promised to
give you an opportunity to take an examination for a medical
licence. Now he is gone – gone from all of us!'

Mr Oh sat silent, with lowered head.

'I have given serious thought to your future,' Mrs Baek
continued. 'I have no influence or authority to aid you, Mr
Oh. I hope you understand. What do you think about going
back to your hometown in the country? I understand you have
no immediate family there.'

Mr Oh maintained his silence.

'We'll stay here for a short time,' Mrs Baek said calmly. 'I'm
afraid I have no choice but to sell this house and move on. If
the clinic is completely empty without you, Mr Oh, I'm
concerned about my daughter. She might be scared of this
place. I wish you could stay a little longer and keep the place
for a while, even though we do not receive patients any more.
Please don't mind me, Mr Oh. It's merely my wish, and I
know I have no right to ask you to stay for a while.'

Still Mr Oh made no response. Mildly surprised, Mrs Baek
looked at him for a while. Mrs Baek, who had been a doctor's
wife, even imagined Mr Oh might be suffering from the first
stages of some trauma. Finally, Mr Oh opened his tightly shut
mouth, and said, 'I appreciate what you have just said, but
just now I have a problem.'

Mrs Baek listened to him silently.

'To tell you the truth, the fire chief, who has gone insane, is
proving a headache.'

'What are you talking about?'

'He has come here several times in the evening to see Dr
Baek.'

'To see Dr Baek?'

'Yes. I tried to explain to him that Dr Baek has passed
away, but he doesn't seem to understand, even though he
attended Dr Baek's funeral himself.' At Mr Oh's explanation
it was Mrs Baek's turn to be speechless.

'Mr Choi has been really stubborn; he said he had

113

something very important to tell Dr Baek. I tried to discourage him from coming inside. I literally had to stand in his way. I talked to him outside, you see.'

Sung-aah's grandmother sighed deeply after listening to Mr Oh.

'What did he have in mind?' Sung-aah's grandmother asked, wiping her eyes. 'My son is gone; why doesn't Mr Choi leave him alone?'

Mr Oh's face became ashen with sorrow and melancholy.

'I wish I knew, ma'am. There is no way to measure a deranged person's mind,' he replied in a lower tone. 'Mr Choi insisted on coming inside. He said Dr Baek was the only person who could understand his problem.'

According to Mr Oh's information, for two nights in succession, Mr Choi had come to see Dr Baek. Sung-aah's mother and grandmother decided to persuade Mr Choi not to come again that night.

'What time does he usually come?'

'He shows up around midnight, ma'am,' Mr Oh replied politely. 'If I don't go outside, Mr Choi stands there all night. I can't sleep thinking of him standing out there all night.'

'It's about ten o'clock now,' Sung-aah's grandmother said, getting up slowly. 'I'll double-check that all the doors are securely locked.'

'Ma'am, I think you should stay inside should Mr Choi come again tonight. He may get more excited if he sees you.'

'It's quite all right, Mr Oh. I'll try to make him understand my husband is dead.'

Although it was too early for Mr Choi to come, Sung-aah's mother and grandmother and Mr Oh went into the clinic through the long corridor connecting the house and clinic. The clinic, once so busy and full of life, looked dreary and deserted without Dr Baek, who used to tend the sick and wounded there. The clinic was so desolate and dark that no one dared to go there alone. As the three of them reached the waiting room that was located by the entrance hall, Mrs Baek stretched out her arm to turn on the electricity.

As she touched the switch, she was dumbfounded to see a face peeping through the window from outside. She was so astonished that she could hardly breathe. The mysterious face, which could be seen through the window, was illuminated by the dim streetlight. It appeared so grotesque as to make one's hair stand on end. The face undoubtedly belonged to Mr Choi. His one big eye kept staring at them, without blinking even once. Without warning, Mrs Baek fainted into her mother-in-law's arms. Swiftly Mr Oh turned on the light and took Dr Baek's cane from its place by the wall.

'Ma'am, please take Mrs Baek inside,' Mr Oh advised wisely. 'I'll take care of him tonight once and for all.'

*   *   *

A few days later, the first snow blanketed the town of Wonjin. The snow accumulated so deep that people had to dig a tunnel in front of their houses in order to pass in and out.

The former fire chief, Mr Choi, was found covered with blood the next morning on the snowy ground. He had committed suicide by cutting his wrist with a razor. The gushes of blood on the snow made a startling contrast.

A few weeks after Mr Choi's suicide, Mr Oh left for his home town, where no one welcomed his reluctant homecoming.

Chapter Four
WINTER

1

Now came the season for snow; it was time to light up each window of the church on the hill late into the night. The gusty wind whistled through the cracks in the boarded wall. At times gritty sleet penetrated into the interior. Yet the atmosphere inside the church was filled with warmth and gaiety. The entire hall was warmed through by people's body heat, the bright electric lights, and the heat from the stove.

Since all the chairs were neatly stacked at one side, the floor had more space. School children of various ages formed each group and were absorbed in their own parts for the forthcoming church play. Some recited the dialogue; others practised dancing; and some rehearsed a pantomime. One group burst into sudden, hearty laughter, accompanying a gleeful conversation; they were quite relaxed and seemed to be enjoying themselves.

The Sunday school teacher and music director, Mr Chang, was conducting a youth choir. His gold-rimmed eyeglasses slipped to the tip of his nose as he led the choir, using a black pencil as a baton. He also used his left hand gracefully in his conducting, and his sharply shaped nose was uplifted as he directed the singing.

'That's right, children, you have to sing this part softly. Remember to sing pianissimo,' Mr Chang narrowed his eyes and contorted his body in keeping with the tune.

'Now, crescendo!' Mr Chang lifted his heels and stretched his shoulders as if trying to touch the ceiling with his baton. At times he turned his body quickly to one side and crossed his arms, forming a large X.

Young-sil's entire attention was captured by Mr Chang's choir. She watched him with immense interest. The youth group to which Young-sil belonged was performing a very important play; consequently, all the members were trying very hard to recite their lines, except Young-sil who had only a small part with the single line, 'Yes, my dear queen'.

Although she had not attended church at all since the spring picnic, Young-sil had had high hopes of being given a star part as a heathen queen who was eventually sent to hell. Naturally, it was out of the question for her to assume that she would have an important part in the play, and she had no choice but to be satisifed to be a lady-in-waiting with just one line to say. Even for this small role, Young-sil had had to compete with quite a few girls. She owed this honour to her aggressive personality – being brazen enough to push herself forward.

Mr Chang finally finished conducting the youth choir and motioned to the church choir members to line up. The entire hall was instantly filled with the majestic, splended chorus of 'Hallelujah!' sung at full volume by the choir, as if they had no concern for other people's privacy. They did not seem to respect others, fully enjoying their sublime chorus. Spontaneously people stopped what they were doing to listen to the beautiful music. Young-sil was one of these admirers; her eyes were wide with respect and wonder.

Young-sil, of course, did not realize it was Handel's glorious Hallelujah Chorus, which should be played in majestic cathedrals. She could not measure the effect of such world-famous music being played in this remote, shabby, boarded shanty church. She could not even imagine how the reverent music touched each heart in the room.

The only thing she was aware of was being carried away by the inspiring music. Her eyes blinded with ectasy, Young-sil felt as if she was ascending into some loftly and pure place. The only times she had this special feeling – clean and entranced – was when she listened to beautiful, breathtaking music. As she stood, enraptured by the music, Young-sil's true nature – coarse, greedy, and selfish – momentarily disappeared. As soon as the chorus was over, other people resumed their business, making noisy remarks. Even after everyone else had settled down, Young-sil was still under its spell. She put one of the chairs on the floor and sat there absentmindedly as if lost in a dream.

Besides adults and children, the floor was cluttered with decorations made of coloured paper. Stars and bells, skilfully cut from silver or green aluminium foil, were scattered everywhere. Small baskets containing more Christmas decorations were much in evidence here and there.

Some workers were busing decorating the Christmas tree with cotton wool ball. Young-sil spotted Bong-chun, the son of the general store owner, absorbed in his task of making a camel pattern on the curtain that would be placed behind the pulpit. He was bending halfway over to do his job, putting brown wool on the pre-paste camel pattern. He was good at this sort of work besides being excellent at the Russian folk dances. The idea that he should dance as part of the entertainment for the Christmas celebration had been presented to the committee; however, the proposal had been turned down after lengthy consideration and discussion by the members.

Even though Bong-chun was aware that he could not perform on the stage, he was eager to lend a hand anywhere he could. As far as Young-sil was concerned, Bong-chun was the only one who attracted her interest among these regular members who came every night to rehearse.

Sung-aah had been pressed to sing a solo, however, she had politely refused. Kyung-sik Yoon, the schoolboy, had gone to Seoul after his father's fatal betrayal of his mother. 'Bukchung Auntie's' son, Chang-kyu, had come only once to watch the rehearsal. He had watched without much interest, leaning against the wall. He did not stay very long before he left and he had never come back.

Young-sil hoped that Chang-kyu might volunteer to play 'Silent Night' on his harmonica. She thought his participation would be eagerly welcomed, as he certainly had a talent for playing the harmonica.

.. Now the rehearsal was at its peak as the night deepened. The characters in the play appeared on the stage. The music

119

director, Mr Chang, and Mr Kwon, who was Mr Chang's junior at the university, were producing and directing the play. Mr Kwon was much younger than Mr Chang; he planned to return to Korea after his graduation the following year. In reality, therefore, Mr Kwon would then be senior to Mr Chang, who still had many years to go before he could graduate.

'Is the organ ready, please?' asked Mr Chang.

'Merchant with camel, it's your turn to appear,' ordered Mr Kwon.

The scenes of the Christmas play progressed smoothly. First a shabbily dressed little girl who was to play the part of an angel, entered and started to sing in a sad tone. Young-sil envied her very much; she would have liked to get this role. However, she gave up upon realizing she could never perform such a role on the stage. The girl had a fair complexion and was very pretty even in her worn-out old dress.

According to the script, the heathen boy took the little girl away, and tried to explain to his queen about the little girl he had just brought. His lengthy explanation to the heathen queen was not going very well; he must have forgotten his lines. He kept stopping to recall what he was supposed to say. As he clumsily repeated his lines, the audience laughed in good spirits, much to the boy's embarrassment.

'Lady-in-waiting, please,' Mr Chang commanded impatiently, realizing that someone was missing. Mr Chang looked around to see whether he could spot Young-sil, who was supposed to be on the stage at this moment. Ignoring Mr Chang's call, Young-sil sat still on her chair without moving an inch. She wanted to watch closely the scene in which the heathen queen ridiculed her servant for his cowardice, laughing coarsely.

The queen got up and took a step forward. She turned round and stood sideways. Without reservation, she laughed aloud.

'Laugh a little louder,' Mr Chang instructed. The queen, played by a girl called Myong-ock who had a round face and was rather plump, laughed louder as she was asked. Her laugh had a fascinating lilt.

'It's time to speak now, dear.'

The queen began to speak. Young-sil tilted her head to listen. Myong-ock seemed to have a natural talent for acting. Her smile was natural and she stood at ease on the stage.

As the rehearsal was repeated, Young-sil took up her role as a loyal lady-in-waiting, standing behind the queen.

'Make a good laugh, please.'

The queen laughed again according to Mr Chang's instructions. Mr Chang, behind the stage, nodded his head as if he were well-pleased with her. At the same time Young-sil noticed Mr Kwon tilting his head as if he were unsure or doubtful of her way of laughing. Young-sil wondered why Mr Kwon seemed to be uncertain – did he think the queen laughed too loud? Or did he think she laughed unnaturally?

'Let's try it one more time,' Mr Kwon yelled. This time the queen laughed with even more gusto. Young-sil did not like the way she laughed; in fact, she hated the way the queen acted with her flirting laugh. When people heard funny stories, they laughed the way the queen had just laughed.

If Myong-ock laughed the way she normally did, Young-sil thought, it would be rather unnatural for the play. How could anyone laugh so naturally, anyway? she frowned. She took a step forward without realizing it.

'Myong-ock, dear, why don't you try it my way?' Young-sil tapped the queen's shoulder and burst into loud laughter. Young-sil's interference did not stop there; she even went ahead with the queen's next line.

'O, you narrow-minded creature. You're no different from those who belived in the prophecy of the wise men from the East!' Young-sil recited the lines in an unnaturally exaggerated tone. Compared with Myong-ock's act, Young-sil's performance was more deliberate – controlled, yet confident – her voice was a lot stronger and louder.

Young-sil's act, strangely enough, sparkled with vitality. Even the initial jeering from people in the audience ceased as she surprised them with her fresh, lively performance. Afterwards, Young-sil returned to her seat and the rehearsal resumed as if nothing had happened.

Whenever Myong-ock forgot her lines, Young-sil spoke out, discouraging her friend from trying further. A few days later, thanks to her brazenly bold behaviour, Mr Kwon decisively gave Young-sil the role of queen. Mr Chang had protested weakly, 'What about her face, though? I don't think she is pretty enough to be queen.'

'No, I don't agree with you,' Mr Kwon had explained patiently. 'I believe her face is perfect for the role. Besides she will be wearing make-up on the night of the play.'

So Young-sil assumed the role of the heathen queen in the play as she had wished from the beginning. Myong-ock, who had to give up her role as the queen, was asked to sing the solo that was originally intended for Sung-aah. Young-sil's heart lept with joy over this small victory – she had got what she wanted. She felt no shame whatsoever for taking the role away from her friend.

Usually most of the people went home straight after the rehearsal. Young-sil, Bong-chun, the good-hearted Myong-ock and a few fun-loving children stayed behind even after the rehearsal was completely over.

'Mr Kwon, please let us hear one of your scary stories,' they begged. The night had deepened long since. Mr Kwon began his favourite story:

'. . . when the stranger opened the door and went inside, he found a man in the centre of the room. Half of the man's body was bumpy stone from his head to his toe. And guess what? The other half was human!'

The children hugged each other, terrified at Mr Kwon's frightening story. Mr Kwon liked to tell the children strange stories. He said his stories are borrowed from the *Thousand and One Arabian Nights*. Young-sil had never heard anything like them before.

The children went outside in groups after Mr Kwon's story was over. The snow-clad road glistened by the light of twinkling stars. The boisterous children took an alley which was dimly lit by surrounding houses. The pale light seemed a lot warmer than the cold starlight. It was difficult to identify anyone in his thick winter clothing; most children's necks and chins were well protected from the bitter cold with their wool scarves.

'Good night, children.'

'Good night, Mr Kwon.' They cheerfully bade each other farewell for the night.

'See you tomorrow.' One by one the children went on

122

their way. The cold wintry night air was needle-sharp; whenever the wind blew children's cheeks were mercilessly pricked by the cold. Their eyebrows were instantly frozen with the vapour of their breath; whenever they blinked their eyes, their frozen eyelashes made a metallic noise. The severe cold numbed their senses; they could feel nothing in their knees and feet. They moved stiffly like robots that were remote-controlled.

The errand-boy with his bucket took hurried steps towards Mr Chang's father's restaurant. Strong, hot steam came from the restaurant, which specialized in preparing noodles.

Frequently, the children fell down on the ice, which was as strong and smooth as a piece of sheet metal; they laughed heartily whenever someone hit the ice, yet their next steps became even more cautious.

Everyone had gone his separate way now except Young-sil and Bong-chun. If he had gone home directly from church, Bong-chun could have reached his home first. However, he deliberately took a long way round in order to spend more time with his friends on the road, even though his house was only in the street nearest the church.

2

Bong-chun's funny ways of doing his things did not surprise people; in fact, they were accustomed to his unpredictable behaviour. He was usually dull and did not seem to know what he wanted. He loved company; wherever there was a crowd, there he would always be found.

'Good night, Mr Kwon,' Young-sil and Bon-chun said together.

'Good night, all,' Mr Kwon replied.

As Bong-chun and Young-sil passed by the marketplace, the fire station where Soon-hee and her father, Mr Choi, used to live, came into sight across the street.

'I feel edgy,' Young-sil said.

'Why?' Bong-chun asked with a weak smile.

'I went to see Mr Choi's body on that morning,' she explained.

'Did you really? How did he look'

'Covered with blood, you know,' Young-sil trembled slightly and her eyes were dimmed with warm tears. 'Mr Choi cut his wrist with a razor blade. Wasn't it a wasteful and foolish thing to do?'

Bong-chun was speechless.

'I have a feeling he didn't die instantly. I could see a trail of his blood all over the place.'

'What happened to his daughter Soon-hee?' Bong-chun asked in a whisper. Young-sil remained silent. He asked again, in a louder voice this time as if he thought she might not have heard his question.

'I understand Soon-hee went to live with her uncle?'

Bong-chun looked straight at Young-sil's watery eyes, which were nearly covered by her woollen scarf. Suddenly, she stopped walking and stooped down to pick up the end of her scarf. Slowly and deliberately she wiped the tears with the edge of her scarf.

'Let's change the subject, shall we?' she pleaded in a subdued tone.

Bong-chung, apparently at a loss, kept on walking, not knowing what to say to his grief-stricken friend. Both of them in turn nearly fell on the ice. Luckily they had remembered to tie their shoes safely with straw rope which prevented them from falling.

'Look! They're coming this way!' Bong-chun cried suddenly.

'Who's coming? What are you talking about?' Young-sil asked excitedly. They came to a halt. As they stayed rooted to the spot, the distant sound of drums came nearer with the loud chanting of people. Towards them came a strange parade; dozens of Japanese people in line, all wearing some sort of white robes and white cloths on their heads were approaching Young-sil and Bong-chun. They realized they must be the faithful followers of the *saddharama-pundarika sutra* sect of Buddhism. Their manner of dress and solemn demeanour made a bizarre picture on this cold wintry night.

They wore only a pair of straw shoes exposing their bare feet. Their forearms were naked too, and they carried a small fan-shaped drum and a drum stick in their bare hands. Some women could be seen among the crowd. Their deep chanting, as if emanating from beneath the ground, harmonized well with the sound of the drums.

Young-sil and Bong-chung stood stock still, awed, almost frightened at this sudden, strange parade of Japanese Buddhists. Young-sil gave a deep sigh of relief as the commotion of the parade died down. They resumed their walk.

'I remember seeing Hisaya following whenever he saw these Japanese people,' Bong-chun said thoughtfully.

'I understand he wasn't welcome even at his own home,' Young-sil remarked slowly, still in deep thought.

The village people still had no idea or clue what had happened to Hisaya and Chun-mo, the barber's son. As Young-sil and Bong-chun passed by Chun-mo's parents' house, not even a glimmer of light came from the tightly closed windows.

As they entered the wide road, the star-studded darkness of the night seemed to envelop them. Abruptly, something dark moved slightly in the deserted open field. A cat dashed through, brushing past their shoes.

'How would you like me to tell you a scary story?' suggested Bong-chun.

'No, thanks. I don't want to hear any,' Young-sil refused emphatically. He took no notice.

'Anyway, there was once a house there. Do you know why the house was destroyed?'

'Yes, I do know why. Please don't start that story again, now. I mean it.'

'Some time ago there was a man with a mistress who was deceitful and sly. One day the man died of typhoid fever. Instead of burying him in the cemetery, his mistress buried him in the ground just outside the house.'

Young-sil started to cry with fear and frustration, but Bong-chun went on.

'Do you know why his mistress buried him that way? I'll tell you why. He died of typhoid fever, as I said. His mistress had heard that if someone is buried near his own home, he might come back to life. Believing this superstition. . . .'

Young-sil screamed hysterically as she spotted something streaking by on the ice. She desperately clung on to Bong-chun's arm. He chuckled at her, enjoying her terror, and said emphatically, 'This is the spot where he was buried. Right in this place!' He pointed towards it, pushing Young-sil back-wards. She fell down heavily, facing the very place where she thought she had seen something flashing on the ice.

Young-sil had a phobia about ghosts; anything to do with ghosts made her morbidly nervous. Whenever she was overcome by this fear, she could hardly control herself. Nothing could calm her terror, not even the Bible verses and Sunday school lessons she learned at church.

When she was pushed and fell, Young-sil became so dizzy with fear that she temporarily lost her self-control. Now she struggled to get up from the ground. Bong-chung merely stood still watching her. Suddenly, he became stimulated by her appearance. He approached her, wetting his lips.

Once before he had engaged in sexual games with a certain girl, even though it was ridiculous behaviour between a little boy and girl. As he began to fumble at her clothing, strangely enough, Young-sil stayed quite still on the ground. Then, unexpectedly, she lifted her foot and kicked his knees as hard as she could.

At her sudden attack, Bong-chun stepped back and withdrew his hands. She got up swiftly and waited without saying a word. He was afraid of her tongue. He knew how scathing she could be. Surprisingly, Young-sil said nothing. She began to walk away without bothering to shake the snow off her clothes. Bong-chun followed her obediently, thinking he needed to offer her an apology.

As he followed behind her rather hesitantly, he could not see that Young-sil wore a complacent, almost an amiable expression on her face. Bong-chun had not the vaguest idea of her state of mind. It was almost impossible for him to picture Young-sil with a smiling, happy face.

3

'Why don't you go inside, madam? Go ahead. No one is going to stop you.' Young-sil was going to say to the woman who had nearly bumped into her near the main gate. Abruptly, however, Young-sil stopped and turned her head to look at the woman again. The woman, who was standing right by the front gate, was already walking away from Young-sil in great haste. Young-sil could see only her back.

Now Young-sil recalled seeing the same woman near the gate on the last two consecutive days. Young-sil had paid no particular attention to her since so many people had come and gone as the wedding celebrations for Sinn-sil drew nearer. Her memory refreshed, Young-sil turned back and walked boldly towards the woman.

'Who are you, madam?' Young-sil asked, determined to find out who this mysterious woman was. Staring unashamedly, she examined the woman's face with interest. The woman deliberately hid her mouth with a gorgeous, off-white shawl, avoiding Young-sil's bold stare. She tried to walk away from Young-sil; she had a fair complexion and looked refined, indicating that she was from the city. Perhaps she was a liquor dealer, Young-sil speculated. She appeared to be in her early forties, yet she had such a girlish face.

Young-sil was not discouraged or embarrassed in any way in spite of the woman's attempt to retreat from her examination. She stood in front of her and continued to scrutinize her face.

As if she had given up in the face of Young-sil's stubbornness the woman suddenly took her shawl away from her mouth revealing her entire face. Her face looked familiar. 'I know someone who looks just like her!' Young-sil exclaimed to herself. 'Her double eye-lids and delicate mouth – somehow her whole face reminds me of someone; she looks like someone I can't name off hand. Who is it?'

Taking advantage of Young-sil's puzzled state, the woman walked away briskly, nearly pushing away Young-sil with her elbow. She covered her face again with the shawl; she appeared slim and attractive in her serge overcoat as Young-sil watched her from behind.

Young-sil started to walk towards the hilly road in the gathering dusk. She was pensive as if menaced by an unseen omen. Suddenly she seemed to lose all her vitality and energy. The woman had appeared to be gentle and agreeable, yet she could not help feeling uneasy about her.

The danger of walking on the icy, steep road was beyond description. The hilly road had frozen repeatedly, snow after snow. The familiar paths which people had trodden were frozen hard. The surface of the ice had become sturdy and smooth as if a strong and bumpy glass belt had been spread on the road.

An iron chain had been stretched for about six or seven metres along the cliff. The road narrowed as it neared the cliff, and the chain served as a guard rail to prevent slipping and falling. Whenever Young-sil held on to that chain her woollen mitten stuck to it because of the freezing temperature. She walked cautiously, holding onto the chain tightly. Since she hated to go past the fire station, she decided to take a detour in order to get to Sung-aah's house. She took the hilly road which was nearly deserted after sunset.

She was following no particular plan, even though she had intended to go to Sung-aah's house. Before she had had the strange encounter with the mysterious woman, she was on her way to Sung-aah's empty house to look at it once again.

Sung-aah's family had moved to Seoul not long ago. The day before she left, she had directed a warm, friendly smile to Young-sil at school. Encouraged and impressed by this sudden overture, Young-sil went to school the next morning in good spirits. But when she searched for Sung-aah, she was not to be found anywhere. Later Young-sil managed to find out that Sung-aah's family had taken the night train on the evening of the same day that Sung-aah had given her such a friendly smile.

Sung-aah's family wanted to leave Wonjin without being noticed. After they lost Dr Baek so suddenly, they had no reason to stay in this alien town. Young-sil remembered with regret how mean and low she had been to Sung-aah.

A few days later, Mr Chae announced Sung-aah's departure to her class. 'Children, your classmate Sung-aah has moved to Seoul. Her mother came to see me the day before they left for Seoul. Mrs Baek asked me to tell you how sorry Sung-aah was for not being able to say "goodbye" to you all. Sung-aah said she was afraid she might cry. So she left a special message with her mother. Do you understand?'

'Yes, sir,' they said in unison.

When Soon-hee Choi moved down to live with her uncle, Mr Chae didn't bother to let his students know about it. But even though there was no official announcement, his students knew about Soon-hee. Even before Mr Chae informed his students about Sung-aah's transfer to another school in Seoul, they had

128

known about it. The news about both Sung-aah and Soon-hee touched their hearts even though they had a different effect on them.

His students were even aware of the cause of Mr Chae's obvious haggardness; lately his face has been thinner and paler than ever. He looked as if he did not even wash his face before he came to school and had become insensitive to his grooming. He looked dirty and disordered. Children also understood why Mr Chae asked only the students who sat opposite Young-sil to read and write something for him. He deliberately avoided looking at the section where Young-sil sat in the classroom. However, Mr Chae's strange attitude did not bother Young-sil a bit. Instead, she held her head high.

Taking advantage of this golden opportunity, Young-sil played with her friends without feeling guilty. She took full advantage of Mr Chae who appeared unaware of Young-sil's pranks. She even took out a textbook and copied the answers during an examination! Because of this apparently uncontrollable situation, Young-sil caused a great deal of confusion and disorder.

However, considering Young-sil's personality, the loss of Sung-aah had been a great distress and shock. Every day she ran up to Sung-aah's house and looked at it sorrowfully. Whenever she recalled Sung-aah's last touching smile, Young-sil's eyes blurred with tears.

As the sun sank over the horizon, Young-sil left her noisy, crowded house in order to revisit Sung-aah's house and relive her memories of Sung-aah.

Now Young-sil desperately held on to the chain and finally passed by the most dangerous spot. As she walked slowly and cautiously on the icy road, she suddenly felt insecure and uncomfortable. She passed several public bars along the road. From inside glimpses of light appeared mingled with hot steam. The commercial curtain screen on the sliding glass door swayed constantly whenever a door opened or closed. Young-sil could hear the raucous songs of barmaids from within. She caught sight of red and blue dresses through the windows; she heard men yelling harshly. The aroma of food stifled her senses.

Suddenly Young-sil felt a sense of security and warmth near these bars. She completely stopped walking and looked around with fond thoughts. If something were ever to happen to her own father, like Sung-aah's father, Dr Baek, and Soon-hee's father, Mr Choi, or if her mother were to disappear suddenly, Young-sil thought she would know what to do. If something tragic were to take place in her life, Young-sil believed she could take care of herself by working in a bar as a maid. She was sure such a place would ensure her some security. As long as she was near a lot of busy, noisy people, she would not be lonely. She would be all right in this brightly lit place, where hot meals were served all the time. She saw 'Bukchung Auntie' wearing a greasy, sordid apron around her waist, standing by a boiling iron soup pot, her face flushed with heat. She shouted lustily to someone about something. Young-sil could see her facial expression through the window, and somehow she now felt at ease with herself – relaxed and content.

She climbed the wide and not so steep road towards Sung-aah's house. The triangle roof above the entrance hall was hidden by the darkness of night. The pleasantly starched white curtains, which once delighted Young-sil with their crisp feeling, had all been taken down; only dark windows remained, signalling a sense of loss and sorrow in the empty house.

Even the street light and the sign board on the clinic had disappeared. Young-sil remained silent in the street, facing the wall of Sung-aah's house. A fresh idea, that all the doors in the house might not be securely locked, crept into her mind. She approached the small side door that led to the main living quarters. She was afraid that the lonely appearance of the empty main wooden floor and the dark windows of each room would numb her with stalking sadness.

In this melancholy mood, Young-sil gingerly pushed the wooden gate with her finger tip. Surprisingly, the door noiselessly opened inwards as it always did. As Young-sil saw the pitch black inside, she felt instinctively sure that the house was not entirely empty; she felt that someone was standing there. The soft whistling of 'Santa Lucia' could be heard faintly through the night air. Her intuition told her the mysterious whistler must be 'Bukchung Auntie's' son, Chang-kyu. Young-sil was glued to the ground; she held her breath and looked at the front courtyard beyond.

She could dimly make out 'Bukchung Auntie's' heart-breaking handsome son, Chang-kyu, sitting at the edge of the main wooden floor. His profile came into sight. He continued to whistle softly. She could not see his face at all; however, she was positive it was Chang-kyu, judging from his manner of dress and the way he wore his cap on his head. She could picture his expression vividly and clearly in her mind – a sad, pained yet affectionate expression. In fact, she had never seen such an expression on anyone's face; yet she could naturally imagine it on Chang-kyu's face without any difficulty.

As she pictured Chang-kyu in her mind, Young-sil suddenly became engulfed by feelings of indescribable sorrow and melancholy. She could neither explain nor define the nature of the strong feelings that overflowed within her. She stood still by the wooden door waiting for him to finish his song. Her ears gave full attention to the stillness of the night. The stillness, as if it were frozen eternally, lingered in the cold night.

A wave of rage and resentment, surging from the bottom of her heart, swept over Young-sil. She turned round and started to run as fast as she could. As she dashed through the darkness, the straw rope tied round her rubber shoes worked loose and finally became untied. She kept on running in spite of losing the straw rope which had prevented her from falling on the icy ground.

The cold moonbeam shone on the narrow hilly road, which presented the distinctive appearance of a huge glass belt, casting different shades of colour – blue, white, and black. Young-sil passed the chained section of the road without stopping for breath, panting heavily.

Chang-kyu was generally blunt whenever he came across Young-sil on the street; to be exact, he completely ignored her. Young-sil thought she was the only one to be treated coldly; she knew that Chang-kyu was kind and polite to other girls. He was known for liking only pretty girls. 'I know why he's always so aloof towards me. I am not pretty enough to attract his attention,' Young-sil told herself, feeling bitterness inside her. Her intense feeling of rejection was caused by her resentment of Sung-aah rather than her blaming Chang-kyu for his arrogance. 'I won't go to see her house any more, I promise,' Young-sil reassured herself, hating Sung-aah and everything about her.

Young-sil spotted someone standing on the paved road, not very far from the front gate of her house. It was her mother. She was not properly dressed for the cold night. She must have come out hastily in her indoor clothes. Her mother looked around as if she were searching for someone. Then she walked back towards the house. Suddenly she stopped. She appeared to be deep in thought; she turned her head again not caring to look ahead. She kept looking back carefully.

Young-sil, standing stilly by the gate, watched her mother's movements. Her mother looked very tense and edgy; her cat-like light brown eyes turned pale green, flashing in the darkness.

'Here I am, Mum,' she called to her mother as she walked towards the house. Judging from her expressionless face, her mother must have made up her mind about something. She looked at Young-sil and went inside without speaking to her daughter.

Even the front courtyard was brightly lit; all the neighbour women were busying themselves with preparations for Sinn-sil's wedding.

4

Young-sil's house had been boisterous and bustling with activity for the past few days in preparation for Sinn-sil's aproaching wedding. Women had been busy making different kinds of rice cakes and home-brewed rice wine. Now the house was almost deserted; the clamour and excitement in the house had quickly died down; everything had dramatically halted since Sinn-sil had gone to the wedding hall for the ceremony.

Sinn-sil's exhausted parents returned home after the ceremony. Later Sin-sil and her husband Soo-chul Chang dropped in to pay their respects to her parents and left hastily. They came in a private car, its tyres all chained because of the icy road. A few neighbours looked into the house, making it seem even more neglected and unwanted.

Since Sinn-sil's in-laws, the Chang family, were in sole charge of every celebration and feast, Young-sil's house gave the impression of being forgotten. Even the remnants of colourful cloth had entirely disappeared from the house.

For the wedding ceremony, Young-sil was dressed in a traditional dress with a long magenta skirt and lime-coloured blouse. Her short, coarse hair was decorated with a large plastic floral hairpin. Even she was not to be seen at her own house, but perhaps was at the wedding feast at Mr Chang's house.

Some people might have frowned at her or advised her to go home; but probably Young-sil would not care what people might think or say about her. She would have stayed anyway as long as she wanted, regardless of the circumstances. It was likely that she would have stayed for the party even though most of the guests had gone home and the many gates of Mr Chang's house finally had been locked. In fact, she could have stayed for the party until the last minute, and no one would have encouraged her to leave.

In spite of the cold atmosphere in her house, Young-sil's mother busied herself greeting neighbours and offering them something to eat and drink. Even those who had been to Mr Chang's feast came to join the crowd, and by the time night drew near, Young-sil's house had become lively again with noise, laughter and talk.

Young-sil's father, Maan-kap Shin, joined the guests. He did not look well; he appeared to be in a bad mood. Ignoring Mr Shin, the guests entertained themselves with lively conversation. Young-sil's father was not sociable by any means; he did not particularly like to associate with people. The village men shared mutual antipathetic feelings towards Mr Shin; they would rather be left alone than have him for company. Their only reason for this rare visit to Mr Shin's house was Sinn-sil's wedding; otherwise, they would have never have set foot on Mr Shin's property. Those good-spirited men who were mildly drunk from the party at Mr Chang's came to Mr Shin's house for more drinks. They drank without caring and soon got up abruptly to leave in a bad mood. Into the night, Mr Shin was left to drink alone by the small bar.

The room where the women were became noisier as they

talked and giggled. They chatted endlessly as if competing with one another, freely expressing their thoughts and opinions on the wedding.

'I envy you for having such a lucky girl as your daughter,' one woman commented.

'Yes, so do I,' another joined in eagerly. 'Your daughter is blessed with wealth.'

'Your daughter looked like a fairy in the ceremony. I don't think anyone could be fairer than Sinn-sil,' the first woman said emotionally.

'Tell us how you gave birth to such a pretty girl. Tell us your secret, tell us how your conceived that most beautiful girl.'

'You'll have to ask Sinn-sil's father,' another woman teased.

'Oh, my goodness! How could I ask her husband such a thing? You must be joking, my friend.'

The women in the room burst into hearty laughter; they continued to admire Mr Chang's well-to-do, fancy life style in their merriment.

'You made it possible for your daughter to have a good life. I think you deserve a toast,' one woman suggested. Young-sil's mother received a small wine cup gracefully and drank it obediently. She neither smiled nor looked happy, yet she honoured her friends' request by drinking some wine. As they looked into her green eyes more closely, some of the women noticed that now and then her eyes were misty with tears. Yet they refused to stop talking; in fact, they deliberately continued their boisterous conversation.

After she finished clearing the tables with the help of several women, Young-sil's mother noticed that her husband was not to be found anywhere in the house. She went to the kitchen and sat curled up like a cat in the tiny room. The aroma of food and body heat of people still lingered in the kitchen. She was the only one in the house now. Everyone had gone.

It was well after midnight when Young-sil finally returned home.

'Am I sleepy!' she said drowsily, ready to lie down by her mother. She looked at her mother's face and suddenly got up and went to Sinn-sil's room. Instantly, she fell into a heavy sleep, breathing regularly.

Young-sil's mother got up swiftly from her bedding and went to each room in the house – Sinn-sil's old room, the back

134

room, and a small room attached to the veranda – and peered into each of them to see if her husband was there. She had had a sudden feeling that her husband had returned noiselessly, but he had not.

*   *   *

Even though several days had passed, her husband had still not returned. Day after day Young-sil's mother looked after those who came to celebrate the happy occasion of Sinn-sil's wedding. She received every guest kindly, offering good food and wine in her poised, quiet manner.

Whenever she was left alone, she always returned to sit by the large iron cooking pot in the kitchen. No one seemed to notice or suspect Mr Shin's sudden disappearance. Since he was regarded as a loner, no one thought his disappearance strange. Even if he was at home, he seldom made himself known. Enveloped with hidden anxiety, Young-sil looked down at her mother who sat motionless by the cooking pot. One evening as she watched her mother sitting all alone in the kitchen, a strange idea alarmed her.

'Yes, that's it. I have an idea,' Young-sil exclaimed quietly yet triumphantly.

Young-sil's long magenta skirt, which she had worn on her sister's wedding day, was already dirty and crumpled, and its hem was beginning to roll up from her carelessness. Her padded cotton bloomers, which were rolled up to her knees so as not to be seen under her skirt, had come loose on one side, covering her calf.

Young-sil had been gazing down at her mother, whose round face had become deeply furrowed of late. She still had a good complexion, yet it was shadowed by unspoken worry and anxiety. As she watched her mother intently, Young-sil recalled the face of someone who was totally different from her mother. She was remembering the encounter with the mysterious woman not long ago. That woman had a fair complexion and looked quite stylish even though she hid half of her face with her delicate shawl. Young-sil could clearly picture her double eyelids and the curving shape of her mouth.

'I know what it is. She looked like Sinn-sil! Yes, that's it – she looks just like my sister,' Young-sil exclaimed excitedly.

At her daugher's excited words, Young-sil's mother moved slightly as if to acknowledge her daughter's remark.

Young-sil was surprised at herself, blurting out such an irresponsible remark so lightly. She opened her eyes widely with mild shock and looked at her mother. Her mother was still sitting straight as before without moving. Young-sil was extremely embarrassed, realizing her fatal mistake, yet she had to go on.

'Mother, that woman who I saw the other day near our house, looked just like my sister. Do you think she could be Sinn-sil's mother?' Young-sil blurted out without considering for a moment the implications of her remark. Once she was haunted by such suspicion, she could not control herself. She became very excited and talkative.

'Mother, I'm sure the woman must have come to see her daughter get married. I bet she runs a bar in Pyongyang or in Seoul.'

Young-sil's mother was still speechless.

'I know what I'm talking about, Mother. I bet that's why the woman was hanging around the main gate the other day!'

She became quiet for a while, still thinking about what she had said.

'Maybe not,' she said more loudly this time, 'I don't think the woman came to see Sinn-sil. She came to see Father, not Sinn-sil.'

This time Young-sil was astonished at her own comment; she abruptly stopped talking as her mother turned her head to look at her. Young-sil noticed with a feeling of unreality a string of tears trickling down her mother's cheeks. Her mother was weeping. Big tears rolled down her cheeks from her light brown, at times green, expressionless eyes. Young-sil had never dreamed of actually witnessing her mother weep. She was so amazed she could not even feel sorry or sad for her mother. Instead, she was overwhelmed with a strange sensation. She fell deathly silent, went to the corner, where she did not have to face her mother and lay down, curling up like a baby.

*   *   *

The following day Young-sil's father, Mr Shin, returned. As soon as he entered his room, Mr Shin threw down his black overcoat lined with wool on the floor and without a single word lay down, putting his overcoat over his face.

Young-sil peeped into the room through the crack in the door to see her father. His worn-out overcoat was all wet, presenting an impression of sordidness and carelessness. She easily guessed why his overcoat was so dirty – he had been walking around aimlessly in the snow. His winter shoes lined with wool looked frozen.

Mr Shin slept until dusk, snoring heavily. He got up sometime after nightfall and sat still for a long time, facing the wall. Suddenly he put on his overcoat and went outside in a flurry. As Young-sil saw her father leaving again she went to the room attached to the kitchen and shook her mother.

'You'd better go after Father. Please, hurry up, Mother! Otherwise, you'll lose him again.'

In spite of Young-sil's obvious concern and excitement, her mother still sat tightly like a tumbling doll; she did not even blink her eyes.

'Aren't you going to follow him? If you don't, Mother, I have nothing more to say to you,' Young-sil said in a louder, more agitated tone. Her mother remained unresponsive.

'Please go quickly. If not, that other woman will steal your husband from you, can't you see that?'

Immediately Young-sil regretted what she said. She felt uneasy using the phrase 'other woman'. She was afraid her mother would be hurt by her tactless, careless words. However, she soon convinced herself that there was no time for such idle worry. Her mother's apathy infuriated her.

'I've told you everything you ought to know. Aren't you going out to find him?' Young-sil yelled frantically, roughly pushing at her mother's head. Her mother was pushed backwards, lifting up her legs.

Without looking back at her mother, Young-sil rushed outside. The crescent moon in the sky greeted her. She ran in the same direction which the woman had taken when she disappeared. The icy road was quite dangerous even to walk on, never mind to run on. She ran fast regardless. She could see nothing beyond; she just kept on running, however, not knowing when or what to expect to see.

Young-sil passed the barbed wire strung along behind the military police post. The post was notoriously frequented by ghosts. She also dashed by the little witch's hut and the willow tree where the woman had hanged herself. She ran by the gloomy school buiding and slowed her pace as she reached the foot of Chunma Mountain. She kept walking briskly until she set her feet on the street that led to the seashore. Not even once had she fallen on the icy road in spite of her wild running.

She met several people on the road, but she had no time to acknowledge any of them. As if she had a great secret, Young-sil quickened her pace. Now she understood why her.father's overcoat and shoes were soaked. It wasn't just from the snow. Judging from his salty, fishy smell, Young-sil realized her father had been to the seashore. Even though she was not positive about her speculation she subconsicously felt confident that she knew where her father had been for the past few days.

The sight of many small steamboats and fishing boats on the beach greeted Young-sil as she neared the shore. Since the edge of the sea was frozen hard, most boats where pulled on to the beach; some were still afloat, anchored a distance from the shore. The large steamboat that sailed to and from Wonjin to Shinho, Japan, and other large ships were secured at the quay near the brothel district.

The shore she was approaching was used mainly for fishing vessels. The fishy smell seemed to be frozen in the air. Empty fishing nets flew freely in the cold wind, completely detached from those busy, golden hours of bountiful catches of pollack and sardines from the sea.

Young-sil approached the breakwater, passing by the sandy beach, crisp with frost. From the dam, shabby freighters and steamships left for neighbouring harbours, carrying fish or other cargoes; at times, those boats also carried passengers.

The steamboat must have already departed. The breakwater was empty. The whistle of the vanishing steamboat was growing fainter as it steamed away in the dusk. Young-sil returned to the beach and walked along the shore, watching the disappearing boat. Presently she came to the big rock on which Kyung-sik once lay. Abruptly Young-sil stopped walking as she spotted someone dressed in black sitting on the sand. The heavily built man, who wore a woollen cap and black overcoat, was sitting on crossed legs on the sand, fiercely pouding the sand with his fist. He wailed miserably as he hit the sand. The sound of his crying tore at her heart, yet at the same time Young-sil jeered at his emotion. She watched his movements from an odd angle. The cause of her contempt for her father had nothing to do with her love for her mother. Somehow she felt triumphant at her father's defeat; it gave her a sense of victory.

So, finally the woman had gone, the woman who resembled her sister Sinn-sil, the woman who was so pretty and refined had left in the steamboat. As Young-sil sneered again, her father unexpectedly got up and ran towards the bathing beach, still wailing sadly. He faced the sea. His overcoat flapped in the sea wind, making a loud noise. He ran fast, raising his arm with his fist tightly clenched, as if he were angry at the sea. Stepping on the ice at the edge of the sea, he waded into the water.

As she watched her father, Young-sil was gripped with sudden fear for him. She followed him, racked by a mixture of intense feelings – apprehension, confusion, contempt, pity and love.

Her father was still crying to the silent, dark sea.